P1

Journeys with Fortune

Elizabeth Bodien's captivating exploration of her past-life experiences will entice and engage you from page to page. Through her warm and vibrant writing, we experience the rich possibilities these explorations open to her in her understanding of her present-day self and life. Her innerworld voyaging offers her a larger sense of her own, and by implication, all our lives. Wherever you feel yourself on the spectrum of belief or acceptance, no matter! You will find yourself held in the grips of her lively, vivid telling until the last page.

-Judyth Hill, author of *Dazzling Wobble* and *Finding the Midline: How Yoga Helps a Trial Lawyer Make Friends and Connect to Spirit*

A fascinating glimpse into one seeker's exploration of her past and future lives under the watchful care of her spirit guide, Fortune. Well-written in a clear and candid style, the author weaves a delightful story that eases the reader through complex and multilayered realities. Vivid first-person accounts of Bodien's other lives evoke pathos as the reader experiences their sorrows and triumphs. Fortune is an ever-present spirit who offers insight and perspective on the unfolding journey. His wisdom and wit bring a levity to a tale that otherwise might seem strange and unreal to those unfamiliar with the subject. *Journeys with Fortune* is wonderfully confirming and inspiring, especially for readers who are new to the study of past lives and who wish to delve deeper into their own journeys.

-Rev. Judith Rochester PhD, author of *To Touch the Soul: How to Become a Medium*

Journeys
with
Fortune

A

Tale of

Other Lives

Also by Elizabeth Bodien

Blood, Metal, Fiber, Rock

Oblique Music: A Book of Hours

Journeys
with
Fortune

A
Tale of
Other Lives

Elizabeth Bodien

ROCHESTER, NY

Cover and book design by Nina Alvarez
Author photo by Elaine Zelker, LLC

For permission to reprint portions of this book, or to order a review copy, contact editor@cosmographiabooks.com

ISBN: 978-1-7322690-6-4

For Andrew,
who opened the door

Was it light?
Was it light within?
Was it light within light?
Stillness becoming alive,
Yet still?
A lively understandable spirit
Once entertained you.
It will come again,
Be still.
Wait.

-from "The Lost Son" by Theodore Roethke

I knock at the stone's front door.
"It's only me, let me come in.
I don't seek refuge for eternity.
I'm not unhappy.
I'm not homeless.
My world is worth returning to.
I'll enter and exit empty-handed.

And my proof I was there
will be only words,
which no one will believe."

-from "Conversation with a Stone" by Wisława Szymborska

You are apple trees in full flush, doors of the temple open,
the polish of marble.
It's the rub of love—tectonics of dream—
how, ardent, we can constellate into ancient shine.

-from "100 Views of the Floating World" by Judyth Hill

Contents

Prologue 13

1. As Rita in Mexico 15

2. *Interlude:* Meeting Fortune 50

3. As Susan in England 65

4. *Interlude:* With Fortune 96

5. As Bethany in Helvetia 101

6. *Interlude:* Conversation with Fortune 130

7. As a Sandal-Maker in Ancient Greece 137

8. A Very Early Life 162

9. *Interlude:* Again with Fortune 177

10. As Pieter, the German Calligrapher 182

11. *Interlude:* Fortune's Directive 219

12. As Orcus in Old Jerusalem 229

13. As a Priestess-in-Training in Atlantis 261

14. As Syzzyx in a Future Life 298

Epilogue 320

Prologue

What seems at first like an accidental meeting can later prove to be pivotal, even life-transforming. Such was the case when my friend, Andrew, was curious about past-life work and I arranged to see the hypnotist Tom Thomason on Andrew's behalf. I had no way of knowing at the time that such a meeting would turn into years of exploring past lives. I can say that I am immensely grateful that such things can and do happen and that, thanks to Andrew and to unseen presences as well, my life expanded as it has.

I have glimpsed beyond the material world of physical objects and creatures of Earth. The unseen presences—guides, spirits, the dead, and so forth—have led me to see that my familiar world is such a small part of all that is. Maybe we don't just live these little lives from birth to death, but any number of forms of existence between and beyond. To have learned something of those planes has enhanced how I understand the pushes and pulls of my present familiar life—my work, my relationships, my personality, my dreams.

I changed the names of some people to protect their privacy, but the transcripts of my past-life regressions have been faithfully transcribed from the original tapes.

I invite you, dear reader, into what was quite an adventure for me—an adventure that had me questioning the nature of existence as I knew it and ultimately expanding my perspective in unexpected ways.

Chapter One
As Rita in Mexico

Let me begin where I began that first day: with doubt. As I drove that warm summer afternoon to the home and office of Tom Thomason, a past-life hypnotist, the most pressing thought in my mind was: *Why am I doing this?* I had read about reincarnation during studies in world religions. I had even lived in different parts of the world among people for whom reincarnation was an unquestioned fact. But I certainly wasn't aware of having lived any past lives myself and had declined previous invitations to explore such possibilities. The way I saw it, I had enough to keep me occupied in my present life without trying to take on other lives.

But I couldn't help wondering what implications such a meeting might have for me. Even though the hypnotist's secretary had assured me when I made the appointment that I wouldn't be called on to do anything that felt uncomfortable, I was more than a little nervous. The house looked reassuringly ordinary though, and the older man who opened the door welcomed me warmly enough. He introduced himself and told me he'd just be a few minutes finishing a previous appointment.

As the previous client was leaving, I scrutinized him to the limit of politeness. If his session had produced any remarkable effects, they were not visible to me.

When my turn came, Tom answered my questions

patiently as I sat on a couch opposite him. He had worked for many years as a more traditional psychologist, he explained, but found that people's problems could not always be traced to sources within their present lifetimes. If one did carry problems from one lifetime to the next, he speculated that there might be a chance of finding answers or at least clues in the patterns of past lifetimes. In his practice he had found this to be the case; people did seem to find relief from their otherwise intractable problems.

What he said made sense in a certain kind of way, but I still felt uneasy about allowing myself to be hypnotized. I wondered if I would say or do ridiculous things or reveal intimate details of my private life. I had seen stage hypnotists who, by simple suggestion, made their subjects collapse onto strangers or onto the floor in front of an audience. That kind of exploitation always made me feel extremely uncomfortable.

However, in this situation, there was no audience other than Tom, and he assured me that his purpose was not to make spectacles of people, but to help them sort out their lives. He also pointed out that, although hypnosis has the effect of relaxing the conscious mind, it does not usually eliminate the conscious function entirely. Part of the self remains well-aware of what one is doing or saying. Moreover, there would have to be extreme conditions, including severe sensory deprivation, for this ongoing consciousness to be threatened.

I asked why hypnosis was necessary to learn about past lives *(assuming there are such things as past lives,*

I thought to myself). Tom explained that the mind relegates all such memories to the subconscious level because they would be too much for the conscious mind to handle. The amount of information and intensity of emotions connected with past lives would overwhelm the conscious mind. So our minds actually protect us by controlling our access to these buried experiences. However, hypnosis can, for a brief period, allow a person to slip past the vigilant conscious mind and explore the deeper recesses. Though vast areas of memory remain untouched in the process, what is uncovered may have a significant relationship to one's current life.

Not that hypnosis is the only means to discover past lives, Tom explained. Seeing a place or a person known in a previous lifetime might spontaneously trigger bits and pieces of memories in some people, even in their normal mode of consciousness. (I wondered if some of the experiences we call déja vu might be explained this way.) Meditating with the intent of remembering past lives may also produce positive results.

"Now, you haven't been hypnotized before, correct?" Tom asked.

"Not knowingly or intentionally." I wondered whether some forms of advertising I might have been exposed to counted as hypnosis.

"But you have done meditation and similar things?"

"Yes."

"Well then, just lie down and make yourself comfortable before we start."

As I arranged myself on the couch, Tom adjusted

the microphone and tested the equipment he would use to record the session after the initial induction routine. I wondered if he avoided recording the induction in order to prevent people from trying to do the process themselves. Later he explained that it would just be a waste of recording anyway since the content of the session would no doubt be more important than how one got into it.

He began by guiding me through a long, pleasant relaxation and visualization routine. He told me to go to a past life that had the most to teach me about my present one.

My present life did not include any major life-threatening concerns. I was a single mother of a young son. I was dating occasionally but there was no one special relationship at the time. I was working as a graphic artist that, being only part-time work, allowed me to care for my son. There was not any reason for me to seek out a past-life hypnotist or any kind of therapist to help solve problems. However I was curious as to whether any relationships with men I had spent time with would develop into something more serious. I did have vague concerns about whether my part-time work would provide sufficiently in terms of both finances and personal challenge. And I was quite naturally concerned as a mother about my son, though he seemed to be doing okay. So here I was, motivated by curiosity more than anything else to see what might happen.

Concentrating on Tom's instructions, I wondered if and when I would start feeling different. Though I didn't know exactly what to expect, I thought there were bound to be some noticeable change.

Tom told me to step into a tunnel, gave a few other instructions, and then told me to step out of the tunnel into a past life. At that point, with my eyes closed, I could hear Tom turning on the recorder. He began asking me what I was experiencing. He said, "You are now there. You are now fifteen years of age in your previous lifetime. I want you to look around and, speaking in a loud, clear voice, tell me: Where are you? Are you indoors, or are you out-of-doors?"

I answered, "Outdoors."

"Okay. Can you tell me: are you male or female?"

"Female."

"Can you speak just a little louder for me, please? How are you dressed?"

"A white . . . white dress on."

"Is it a long dress to the ground, or is it shorter?"

"Short. To the knees."

At this point I realized I was two people simultaneously. I was this strange, barefoot, dark-haired girl—and at the same time my familiar, and very different, rather blond, rather middle-aged self, lying on the hypnotist's couch and answering his questions. When I became aware of being two very different people at the same time, I became curious about this other person who was also supposedly me.

"What is your name? Just open up your mind and tell me whatever thought comes in."

"Rita."

When Tom, the hypnotist, suggested I just say whatever came to mind, the name Rita surfaced from somewhere in two separate syllables, sounding at first like "Li-ta." It did take a moment before I could come up with the name. And into that moment, the mind of my present self quickly intruded, telling me I must be making up the whole story. Surely if it were real, I would know my own name! This kind of monitoring of my past mind by my present mind continued throughout the session as a sort of editorial comment on what I was experiencing.

"Do you know what country you live in, Rita?"

"No."

"Do you live with your family?"

"Yes."

"Are you out in the countryside or near your home? Can you describe where you are at this moment?"

"Not far from the home."

I was seeing a few trees now. The ground was flat and dry, barren of grass. Though I could not actually see my home from where I stood, I knew how to find my way there. I knew it was a small, earthen building with open spaces that served as windows in the thick clay walls.

"Do you know what year it is?"

"No."

Why couldn't I answer this question? Again my skeptical present mind intruded, thinking I ought to be able to come up with a year. Who was this Rita anyway? Perhaps just a figment of my imagination?

When Tom asked about being indoors or outdoors, I

couldn't see any walls so I said, "Outdoors." But since I, in my present mind, knew that I was indoors, I thought I was probably just making that up too. When asked whether I was male or female, I still wasn't convinced my answer came from another lifetime. However, when he asked what I was wearing, I looked down at myself, not with my physical eyes (which were closed), but with my mind's eye. My appearance as Rita—the short, white dress, long disheveled black hair, and bare feet—had nothing at all to do with my present appearance. I was fascinated but skeptical.

"All right. I want you to move forward in time now. On the count of three, I want you to move to a time when you are with your family, in your own home, without any stress or tension. One . . . two . . . three . . . You're now in your home. Is your family there with you—your mother and father?"

When I heard Tom say the word "family," my present mind assumed he meant a family in which I would be the wife and mother. But as soon as Tom said the words "mother and father," I got a clear picture of all of us in the past life.

"Yes, we're sitting around a table."

"Do you have brothers and sisters?"

"Little ones."

"Are you the oldest child?"

"I think so. I take care of the others."

"How many brothers and sisters do you have?"

"One . . . two . . . three . . . maybe. I think there's going to be another one."

"I see. And you're how old?"

"About sixteen or seventeen."

The answer about my age seemed to come from my present mind looking into the past life rather than from Rita herself.

"What are your mother's and father's names?"

"José."

"Mm-hmh."

"My mother's name is Rita too."

"I see. Would you ask your mother what country you live in, please?"

"She says Mexico."

"All right. Ask her what year it is."

"She says I ask too many questions."

I, as Rita, didn't like asking my mother these questions because I didn't quite understand them and I wasn't in the habit of asking her such things. Therefore, I wasn't surprised at her annoyance. In fact, she seemed permanently annoyed with me, though I didn't know why.

"Tell her you need to tell a friend of yours. It's very important."

"She says to ask my father."

"All right. Ask your father what year it is."

"He isn't there. He hasn't come home."

"I see. Are you a happy young lady?"

Hesitatingly, "Yes."

"Do you live in a nice home? Are you fairly wealthy or . . . ?"

"Not so wealthy."

Actually, we were downright poor, but I had only recently become aware of the fact. I was getting uncomfortable with these questions. My present mind could handle them easily enough, but not my past-life mind.

"What's your last name, your family name?"

"Gomez."

"Do you know what city you live in?"

"No, but it starts with (the sound) 'h'—"

"Ask your mother."

"Huaca . . . something like Huaca . . . Guahuaca."

"Huaca. On the count of three, I want you to move forward to a time when your father is in the house and you're able to talk with him without any stress or tension. One . . . two . . . three . . . Your father is now in the house. Ask him what year it is, please."

"He says I should take care of the children and not ask questions."

"Tell him that it's important, that a friend of yours asked and you need to tell him."

At this, I sensed my father had several other unspoken concerns. He looked at my mother as if to ask what was going on and whether she knew who this "friend" was. He was obviously unsettled by my questions and looked uncertain about coming up with an answer.

"He says, '17 . . . 17 something. 1749.'"

"Okay. What does your father do?"

"He works . . . for a very wealthy man."

"On a plantation?"

I was momentarily irritated with Tom's choice of the

word "plantation" because my present mind connected that word with plantations in the pre-Civil War South of the United States, plantations which looked very different from this, although the word itself correctly described both places.

"He works in the fields."

"Have you ever had to work in the field?"

"No. I just take care of the children."

"Does your mother work in the field?"

"Sometimes when I'm taking care of the children she goes with my father."

"Are you a pretty girl?"

"Yes."

"Do you . . . uh . . . have any boyfriends?"

"No."

"What do you do when you're not taking care of the children? Have you ever gone to school?"

"No."

"Do you go to church all the time?"

"No. Just sometimes."

"Do you enjoy the church?"

"I like the music."

Here a wave of pleasure swept through me as I felt the sound of the music waft through the high reaches of the church. The tone of my voice reflects this wonderful feeling, a far cry from the monotonous tone of the rest of the past-life voice. I saw the church clearly: large and pinkish-white, with two large towers and two big crude wooden doors in the middle of the façade with steps leading up to them. The church had a solid, permanent feeling, as if it had been there longer than anything else and would continue forever. It fronted on a town square or plaza. Nothing in the vicinity was anything like it in size, grandeur, or importance.

"Is the Father nice to you?"

"Yes, he says I'm a good girl."

My voice here sounded innocent. I think the priest said I was a good girl because I looked after the younger children without much complaint. Though I knew it was part of his role to say such things, I was always pleased to hear them anyway. It felt good to have some support from any corner even though I sensed that my own "goodness" was of less use to me than to others, especially my mother.

"Can you talk just a little bit louder, please? So that it's easier to record."

My present mind noticed the reference to recording and realized that it was clearly a comment referring to something only my present mind could understand.

"Unless there's something of importance, I'd like to have you move forward in time. On the count of three. To where you are eighteen years of age. One . . . two . . . three . . . Where are you now?"

"Just outside the church in the village."

"What is happening?"

"I'm arguing with my mother."

"About what?"

"She says I should come home and I don't want to come home."

"What do you want to do?"

"I want to go with my friends."

"What are they going to do?"

"They're going to the festival. They want me to come. My mother says I should stay with the children."

"She doesn't want you to have much of any life of your own, does she?"

"No."

"All right. Let's move forward in time 'til you make a decision whether you go with your mother or to the festival. Where are you now?"

"I go to the festival."

"And what happens there? Do you have a good time?"

"Yes."

"What do you do?"

After the argument with my mother, my resentment of her intrusion into what should have been my private life seemed to carry over as a reluctance to reveal to Tom details about what I then did with my friends. Tom and my past-life mother shared for the moment a common role as authority figures that I resented having to answer to. Neither did I want to talk about Rita's own feelings about what was happening. Though I was old enough by now in the past life to understand some of the conflicts I was experiencing, I didn't have either the vocabulary or the psychological sophistication to discuss them.

"There's a dance and we dance. There's music."

"Do you enjoy dancing with the boys?"

"Yes. Lots of colored papers . . . colored papers."

The colored papers were streamers that hung from

poles around a smaller secondary plaza behind and to the left of the church, as one faced it from the main plaza. Watching the streamers blow in the wind while I was dancing made me dizzy.

The dancing, for the most part, was circle dancing in which boys and girls interested in each other would single each other out with their eyes. So, when asked if I liked dancing with the boys, I realized I wasn't just enjoying dancing with boys in general, but was preoccupied with one boy in particular.

My reluctance to answer came out of a feeling that Tom was getting ahead of me. Also, I wasn't sure whether it was okay for me to enjoy dancing with boys or with any one boy in particular, so perhaps my talking about the colored papers was designed to deflect Tom's questions.

"Do you drink a little wine?"

"Drinking something."

"Are you feeling very good?"

"Yes, but I'm worrying about the children."

I was genuinely worried about the children, but also worried about my responsibility for them. After all, I had stubbornly taken off on my own for the first time, and was enjoying myself in the process.

"Well, can't your mother take care of them? This is a Sunday, isn't it. When you've been to church?"

"No. It's not a church day."

"Oh, I see. But it must be a holiday of some kind if they're having a festival, right?"

"They have it every year."

My voice at this point had a slight know-it-all

smugness because I now felt knowledgeable and in control, whereas up to this point I had felt myself led by Tom's questions.

"Every year at this time, hmmm. Do you have a special boyfriend?"

"There's one boy I like."

"Has he ever kissed you?"

"No. We danced."

"I see. Anything else you'd like to tell me or shall we move forward a little bit in time?"

"Let's move forward."

Tom's reference to moving forward immediately catapulted my attention from the past life to the present one. Whenever procedural aspects of the regression session were mentioned (such as moving forward in time or speaking louder to record better), I felt as if I had moved up from some deep-sea-like realm of the past life much closer to the surface of my present life.

"You're now eighteen years of age. I want you to move forward to where you're twenty unless there's something special that has happened in the meantime. If it has, go there. One . . . two . . . three . . . Where are you now?"

"One of the children died."

"I see. And without any stress or emotion now, simply as though you were an observer: Was the child sick?"

"No. He ran over a cliff."

"When he was playing?"

"He didn't know. He wasn't watching."

"How old was he?"

"Four."

"Did your parents blame you for it?"

"Yes."

"Were you responsible or just that they all were playing and you were watching all of them?"

"I wasn't watching any of them."

"What were you doing?"

"I was with my friend."

"Your boyfriend?"

"Yes."

"And what were you doing?"

"Out walking together. I was supposed to be watching the children."

"And you feel very bad and guilty about it?"

"Yes."

"Are your parents going to let you live there still?"

"I don't know."

"Let's move forward a month in time until the decision is made, on the count of three." One . . . two . . . three . . . What is happening now? Are you still living at home?

"Yes."

"Are things better now?"

"No."

"Are you very unhappy?"

"Yes."

"Are you spending more time with your boyfriend now?"

"No, not at all."

"Are you ashamed to be with him because you felt so guilty about what—"

"Yes." I was on the verge of tears.

"Do you take care of the children all the time now?"

"Yes."

With resignation, I looked ahead to a miserable and colorless future that stretched as far as I could see in front of me.

"Do you ever want to get married and have a family of your own?"

"I don't think I can."

"Why?" He paused. "You are a beautiful girl, aren't you?"

"Yes."

"And men find you attractive?"

"Yes."

With the second of these yeses, my vocal pitch became much lower, reflecting perhaps a change from girlish to womanish feelings in relation to men. Though I was aware I was beautiful, I was not self-conscious about my beauty and certainly never did anything to enhance it.

"All right. Anything else you want to tell me? Do you feel like you want to leave home or do you want to stay there?"

"I don't know."

"All right. On the count of three, I want you to move forward to where you are twenty-two years of age. Without any stress or tension, letting go of all of this behind you. One . . . two . . . three . . . Where are you now?"

"I'm in a big city."

"What are you doing there?"

"I'm in the market. I'm trying to sell some things."

"I see. What kind of things?"

"Some fruits and some . . . some fruits and some . . . some peppers."

"Where do you get them from?"

"My father brings them to me sometimes."

Actually, he was stealing them from the fields where he worked, and they were all I had to sell. Though he was my only source, I added the "sometimes" to make it look as though I had other, more legitimate, sources.

"I see. And you don't live at home anymore?"

"No."

"Are you married?"

"No."

"Do you live by yourself?"

"I live in a room by myself. It's with another family."

"Do you eat there?"

"Sometimes. Sometimes I eat at the market."

"Do you have enough money to get along all right?"

"Mmm . . . not so much."

"But you are able to eat and so forth?"

"I eat at the market sometimes. If the things don't sell then I eat some."

"Do you have any boyfriends, or what do you do by yourself?"

"Sometimes I walk in the country. When I don't go to the market, I just walk . . . walk . . . walk."

"Do you still feel very bad about your little brother?"

"Yes."

"Is that in your mind a great deal?"

"Yes." I was aware that I was crying—the present me, it seemed—although I wasn't always separating past and present selves neatly.

"Have your parents ever forgiven you?"

"My father did, but my mother—she got sick afterwards and isn't very well."

"Mm-hmh! Do you think that you may have to go back and start taking care of the children again?"

"Don't want to."

"Have they had any more children since the last one?"

"No, my mother isn't well enough to have more children, I meant to say."

"You're still a very unhappy person then."

"Yes, except my father is good to me."

This was said in a sing-song, little-girl voice, and my present mind, cynically thinking along sexual lines thought, *Oh yeah? Just how good is he?* But whatever may have crossed his mind, nothing like that ever happened.

"He comes and he brings the fruit for me to sell and makes sure I'm okay, but my mother doesn't know."

"Mm-hmh. Then you have nobody to talk to or spend time with. Nobody but your father who loves you?"

"There are some other girls at the market. Sometimes I talk to them but I don't talk to them about how sad I feel sometimes."

My present mind was thinking that I said "sometimes"

too much in the same sentence.

"Why don't you go out with any of the men?"

"I'm afraid."

"Afraid of what?"

"Something bad will happen."

"Well, if there's nobody else around and no children, how could something bad happen?"

I said that I didn't know, but it seemed obvious to my past-life mind that something bad was inevitable.

"Are you . . . do you want to get married?"

"Maybe."

"But if you're going to get married, you have to go out with men, don't you?"

Tom was asking the question from the United States in the current century where marriage customs are decidedly different from those of that past-life place that had no equivalent of the modern practice of dating.

In these sessions, there was always more happening than the recorded dialogue reveals. I had a clear picture in my (Rita's) mind of the marketplace in the main plaza where I sat under the shade of a cloth draped between poles. The girls I talked with sold things in similar stalls around the market but, unlike me, they were always chatty, lively, and flirtatious. Though they liked me and tried to include me in their conversation and social activities, they were either much younger and still unmarried, or older and comfortably settled into married life. I was the same age as some of the older ones but still unmarried.

From my corner of the market, I could see the little

alley that led to the little room where I lived. It was a single spare room with a bed of sorts and my few belongings. Connecting the room with the alley was an outside door. There was also an inside door, up a few steps, which led to the kitchen and the rest of the house where the family lived. Sitting in the marketplace, I kept my eye on the alley, hoping my father would come with more for me to sell, or perhaps with news of a possible husband (although it was something he rarely mentioned).

I knew he wished I could have stayed at home, but my mother was unrelentingly critical and considered me the cause of her decline. Even though he saw the unfairness of this, he couldn't seem to do anything about it. At least I knew he loved me and wanted to support me. Had he mentioned these visits to my mother, I'm sure she would not have allowed them. As far as she was concerned, I had been banished. She had always been jealous of my youth and beauty, and must have thought my being out of sight would also keep me out of my father's mind. My father stayed with this now sickly, complaining wretch of a wife and mother out of duty and kindness. It was clear that he looked forward to our time together as much as I did. I knew he was afraid that if I married, his greatest pleasure in life would be taken from him. We lit up each other's lives, but kept this as much as possible from the rest of the world. I just sat quietly in the market, waiting for his next visit. Watching me from their stalls, the other women seemed to pity my sadness.

Tom continued his probing into the last part of the life I lived as Rita. "All right. On the count of three, I want you to let go of all of this and move forward to where you are twenty-five years of age . . . without any stress or tension. One . . . two . . . three . . . Where are you and what are you doing?"

"Still in the market. I'm still selling things and my mother . . . my mother has died."

"Has died?"

"Yes. She was very sick and she died."

"Do you feel guilty that you caused her to become ill and die?"

"Sort of, but she was sick for a long time."

"Are all of the children pretty well grown-up now so nobody has to take care of them?"

"Just the little ones. The little two. A little girl and boy."

"Does your older sister under you take care of them?"

"My father tries to but he can't. He takes the little one with him sometimes. He says I should come back now."

"I see. Do you want to go back now?"

"No, but I want to help my father. He's been good to me."

"All right. Has he ever found you a man?"

"No."

"Have you ever gone out with any other man during this time?"

"Yes. With the son of the man that he works for."

"Mm-hmh."

"He saw me one day when I went out to find my

father in the fields. He asked my father about me and found out where I was living in the town and came to see me."

"Did you enjoy him?"

"Mm-hmh, kind of, but I think . . . I think I shouldn't be with him."

"Why?"

"I don't think his family would like it. Besides, maybe something bad would happen."

"What would have been bad that could happen?"

"Maybe somebody will die again."

"You're afraid that every time you're with a man that someone will die in your family?"

"Yes."

My present mind was embarrassed by this nonsensical revelation.

"Don't you think that's not being fair to you because you were not really responsible? It was the little boy that ran over and he could have run over even if you were standing just a few feet from him. Isn't that true?"

"Yes, but my mother said it was my fault."

"Yes, but your mother is not God and you can ask God and ask him right now whether you are guilty or not and when we're up with your master we'll find out about that."

I didn't know what Tom was talking about here but chose to let it be.

"All right. Let's move forward another year to where you're twenty-six and see whether you go back or not. One . . . two . . . three . . . Where are you now?"

36

"I'm with the son of the family. Felipe."

"What . . . Felipe? I see. What are you doing with him?"

"We're talking to his father about getting married."

"And what does his father say?"

"He doesn't want to talk about it. He said that before, but he doesn't want to talk about it now either."

"All right. How does Felipe feel about it? Does he still want to marry you?"

"Yes, but he says that it's too much trouble."

"Have you gone out together?"

"Sometimes."

"Do you enjoy him?"

"Yes."

"Does he kiss you and love you?"

"Yes."

"And when you make love, do you enjoy it?"

"Yes."

"And nothing happened, did it? Nobody died, did they?"

"No."

"All right. You're now twenty-six years of age. Is there anything else you'd like to tell me or shall we move forward and see if . . . what happens . . . if you marry him or somebody else?"

"Yes, we're going to get married."

"Oh, you are, huh? All right. Let's move forward to where you are now married to him. One . . . two . . . three . . . You are now married to him. Where are you living?"

"We are living by ourselves. We are living by

ourselves in the town."

"I see."

"Another town. Not where I was."

"What is Felipe doing? Does he get money from his father?"

"He's studying . . . something with the priest he's studying. He goes and he studies."

"Are you happier now?"

"Mmm. Yes. Well . . . yes."

"How long have you been married now?"

"Hmm. I don't know. It was around about six months."

"Do you have enough money so that you don't have to worry about anything?"

"Not so much money, but the priest is making sure we're okay while he is studying."

"Okay. Do you want to have babies with Felipe?"

"Yes, I'm going to have one."

"Oh, you are pregnant?"

"Mm-hmh."

"How soon do you expect to have your baby?"

"Maybe in another few months."

"Were you pregnant when you got married?"

"Yes."

"Is that why Felipe married you?"

"I think so."

"Does he seem to be happy in the marriage?"

"Yes. He likes it."

"Good. All right. How old are you now?"

"Thirty."

"Is there anything else you'd like to tell me or shall we move forward to where you're thirty-five years of age and see what has happened?"

For some reason, I was crying.

"What's the matter now? What is wrong?"

"My baby has died."

"I see. Was it a stillborn baby?"

"Yes."

This was said vehemently and with a catch in the throat. It gives me chills when I listen to the recording of the session.

"Did you have a great deal of difficulty in delivering it?"

"Yes." I said this as I was crying.

"Now, without any stress or tension, just simply as though you were an observer . . . but you're okay now, aren't you?"

"Yes . . . 'cept I don't know if I can have any more babies."

"Well, we'll find out. How is Felipe? Did he take it all right?"

"He was very good. He was very good."

"He's a very kind, loving man, isn't he? And a good husband?"

"Yes."

"And you're a very good wife."

"Yes, but the baby died."

"That happens with many babies, doesn't it?" Tom paused here and then continued. "All right. How old are you now?"

"I'm thirty."

"I see. Let's move forward to where you're thirty-five. At the count of three, unless something of a great deal of importance has happened in the meantime."

"My father died."

"Oh, your father died? How old were you when he died?"

"About thirty-two."

"I see. Most of the children are grown up though now, aren't they?"

"Yes. My sister comes to stay with us sometimes."

"How are you? Is Felipe still studying?"

"No."

"What does he do now? Is he a lawyer . . . or what?"

"He's doing something in the church. He's going to be the priest."

"Is he going to be the priest? How can he be a priest if he's married to you?"

"Well, he's trying. He said maybe he could stay in the church. But it's not the same church. It's a different church. It's in another place . . . and it's a funny church."

"It's not a Catholic church?"

"No."

"Ah! Can you tell me what the name of the church is?"

"It has another name. I don't know that language."

"Is it English? Or American?"

"It's a very, very, old, old, old language. We don't speak that anymore."

In my present mind I noticed that this repetition

of the words "very" and "old" was a childish, or at least unschooled, mode of expression.

"I see. Is it Aztec Indian or Mayan?"

"I don't know. It's very old."

"All right. Let's move forward until you're thirty-five then. On the count of three without any stress or tension: one . . . two . . . three . . . Where are you now?"

"I'm with my sister's child."

"Are you still married to Felipe?"

"Yes."

"Is the child living with you?"

"Yes. My sister's living with us. It's Felipe's child and it's my sister's child and they had a child."

"I see. Did you understand what they were doing and did you agree to it?"

"I didn't like it but I couldn't have any more children."

"And you wanted to give Felipe a child?"

"Yes. And I wanted one myself."

"I see. Does Felipe still make love with you?"

"Not so much."

"Does he still make love with your sister?"

"Yes. He doesn't feel good about it."

"Does he want more children?"

"Yes."

"How about your sister? Is she happy with that?"

"She's going to leave. She's going to take the baby but she's not sure she can take the baby and she wants me to take care of their baby for her. He's about three."

"I see. Do you love the baby as your own?"

"I'm afraid for the baby." This was said very quietly. "I don't want to take care of it."

"Why are you afraid? That you won't take good care of it?"

"Mm-hmh." I was crying again.

This was a big area of conflict for me. Though I wanted to take care of the child, I felt incapable. He was now the same age my brother had been when he died while under my care. My stillborn baby also seemed a clear sign to me that I was unfit to be a mother or to take care of children.

"All right. You're thirty-five years of age now, aren't you? Let's move forward to where you're forty years of age. One . . . two . . . three . . . Where are you now?"

"I'm back in the house I grew up in."

"Are you still living with Felipe?"

"He's gone far away." I sighed. "He's gone far. He's going to do something about the funny church. He says he will come back."

"Do you still have the baby boy that was your sister's and . . ."

"I don't know what happened to the baby."

"Did your sister take it?"

"Yes."

"Where does your sister live now?"

"I don't know."

"You never have seen her since she left?"

"Well, she wanted to do something with the funny church too and she left soon after Felipe left."

"Did she go to Felipe?"

"Maybe. I think so."

"And she took the baby with her?"

"Yeah."

"What are you doing in the house there? Are you living all by yourself?"

"Yeah. Everyone's gone."

"How do you live? Do you get food from Felipe's father?"

"No. People come to me and they tell me things and I tell them things and they like it and they give me money."

"Are you a psychic?"

"Yes."

"All right. If you're a psychic, can you tell me what is going to happen to me in this lifetime?"

"I don't understand."

"You don't understand that?"

I understood Tom's question perfectly well but only in my present mind. The problem was that, though I was able to see the future in that past life, I couldn't understand how I could see for this person whose voice I was hearing now. It was as if I had two lines of communication going at the same time, two mental lines extending from a central point. I was the central point and I could deal both with myself in Mexico (one line) and myself in the present talking to Tom (a second line). But I could not make a connection (a third line or side of a triangle) between myself in the past life and him now. My logic said I should be able to do it, and I certainly felt inclined to help Tom see his future. But it simply wasn't possible.

I have to admit I did feel a flash of resentment at Tom's intrusion into my session but I quickly excused him realizing that, in his shoes, I might have done the same thing. I also thought it possible that his question was some kind of test question related to his research into the process.

"Do you help people when you work with them? And tell them things?"

"Yes, they come and sometimes I can see things through my window that will happen. It's a small window but they come in the evening and I see through my window."

"And you're able to tell them what is going to happen to them in the future?"

"Sometimes, but not so much about things that will happen but I tell them other things and they feel better and they go away."

"What kind of things do you tell them?"

"Oh, I tell them not to worry and I tell them things will be okay and I tell them . . . I tell them they should stay close to the earth." I sighed as I said this.

I would sit at the rough-hewn wooden table, looking out a small window just as the stars appeared in the evening sky. The person I was trying to help would sit across from me at the table, so I could look over his or her head at the stars. I did not focus on any particular formations or constellations but rather had the sense of seeing through the stars. Thus inspired by them, I would know just what to say to help each person. Interestingly, what I said to people then about not worrying and staying close to the earth I would easily say in the present life as well.

"All right. Anything else you'd like to tell me now? Are you happy doing what you do?"

"Oh well, I suppose."

"Do you miss Felipe?"

"Yes, a little, but it's been a long time."

"How many years has Felipe been gone? Since you were thiry-five?"

"Five . . . oh, I've forgotten how many years. It seems like a long time."

"Do you ever make love with any other men? Or do you have any boyfriends? Any men come to see you?"

"Some men come sometimes. They want to hear what I have to say but sometimes they don't really want to hear. They just want to come to make love. They say I'm beautiful, that I should be with a man and they—"

"And do you enjoy it when you make love with them?"

"I don't make love with them."

"Are you . . . is that because you are still married to Felipe?"

"No. They don't come in honesty."

"Anything else you'd like to tell me?"

"I like looking through the window."

"What are you seeing?"

"Stars."

"I see. Can you see what's going to happen to you out the window?"

"No, it seems I should be able to. I can see sometimes

what things will happen, but not about me."

"Can you see something that will happen to me in there?"

"Who are you?"

"Hmm?"

"It's a long time away."

"I see, but tell me what you think you see."

"I don't know." I sighed.

"Okay."

My resistance to Tom's question was the same as before except that this time I was so involved in the past life that I couldn't even see who was asking. There was no one in my room with the window just then. Even so, the question "Who are you?" seemed ludicrous to my present mind because I, as Elizabeth, knew perfectly well who was asking.

"All right. You're forty years of age. Shall we move forward to where you're forty-five and see what happens?"

"I'm not forty-five."

"How old are you?"

"I'm forty-two and I'm an old lady."

"You're forty-two and you're an old lady. Are you still healthy?"

"No."

"Do you feel . . . are you ill?"

"Yes, but I don't know what it is. I shouldn't be ill."

To my present mind, forty-two is still relatively young, but my past-life self was very definitely feeling like an old lady. There was no specific disease, accident or infirmity—more a feeling of aging and fading away.

"Do you feel you're going to die?"

"Yes." There was a catch in my breath here.

"All right. On the count of three, you're going to move forward to the very last day of your life in this incarnation we are now examining. Now remember that you will not have died. You will not have crossed over into spirit but on the count of three it will be indeed the last day in this incarnation we are now examining. Now as an absolute command, you will feel no pain or emotion and you will re-experience this situation objectively and simply as though you were an observer. One . . . two . . . three . . . Where are you now?"

"I'm sitting outside the house . . . sitting under a tree."

"Mm-hmh."

"I don't want to die in the house."

"Are you very ill?"

"Yes, it's hard to go around."

"Going around" consisted of going in and out of the house, depending on where I felt more comfortable temperature-wise. If I was inside in the evening, I would go through my ritual of looking through my window for anyone who came asking for my help. But if I was comfortably settled under the tree, I would try to wave them away.

"And you . . . are you ready to die now?"

"I want to see Felipe again." I started to cry.

"Mm-hmh, but he has never come back, has he?"

"No."

"Has your sister ever come back?"

"No."

"Are you still alone there?"

"Yes, except there's a small girl that comes and she wants to learn from me how to see through the window. She's young."

"How young is she?"

"She's fourteen."

"Have you been able to teach her?"

"I don't teach her, but I think she knows."

"Mm-hmh."

"I think she knows. She watches with me."

"And she sees that you eat and feeds you when you are ill?"

"Yes, she's very good."

"All right. Are you now ready to cross over into spirit?"

"No."

"But you know you are going to, don't you?"

"Yes." There was a clear note of resignation in my voice.

"All right. On the count of three without pain and without emotion, I want you to cross over into spirit, that is, I want you to leave your physical body and find yourself in the spirit world just a few moments after experiencing what we call physical death. One . . . two . . . three . . . You are now in the spirit world."

It sounded like a long series of instructions were in store for me here, but I was grateful for the chance to rest, relax, and listen without having to answer questions.

"Can you see your body in relationship to where you are?"

"It's under the tree."

"Are you looking down at it or are you—?"

"Yes."

"How do you feel now?"

"Free. Free."

"Are you happy now?"

"Yes. I will see Felipe."

"You will see Felipe in the spirit world, won't you?"

"Well . . . sometime again."

Chapter Two
Interlude:
Meeting Fortune

"All right. On the count of three I want you to move forward in time until you are with your master. One . . . two . . . three . . . You are now with your master. Can you feel him and sense him there?"

I wasn't following the instructions very well here because I was still thinking so much about the past life. Somehow I managed to answer Tom's questions anyway.

"And I want you to ask them to show themselves to you, either he or she, and find out what their name is and describe them to me and tell me the name. One . . . two . . . three . . . Is it a male or female spirit?"

"Male."

"What does he look like?"

"Stone."

"Stone?"

"Yeah."

"Is he alive?"

"Yes."

I was laughing lightly. The incongruity of this image struck me as funny. Ever since childhood, I have sensed stones were alive, though in a different way than humans, animals, and plants. Because the stones' pace of life is so slow and their mode so strange, most people simply never notice. Certain land formations, too, have always seemed to me to hold or be held by spirit. I have had many discussions in my present lifetime about this perception of mine, which generally strikes people as bizarre. Needless to say, many have tried to talk me out of it, and I have even tried a few times to talk myself out of it. But the idea has persisted. At the time, I was not aware of the metaphysical properties of different stones, including gemstones, which I learned about later, but I had some sense that stones were more than just inanimate lumps of hard material. Thinking about stones, I had some difficulty pulling my attention back to the session with Tom. The questions he was asking were hard to answer, especially since the abstract realm we were now discussing was harder to describe in normal sensate terms than the past life had been.

"What's his name?"

"Stone."

"Oh, I see. Does he have a beard or what color's his hair . . . or his eyes?"

"It's a stone!"

"It is a stone?"

"Yeah."

"Well, that can't be your master because they're . . . uh . . . "

"It's in the stone . . . in the stone."

"The master is in the stone?"

"I think so."

"Ask the master to come out so you can see the person in the flesh."

There was a pause as someone emerged from the stone.

"Yeah, he's there."

"Can you see them now?"

"Mm-hmh."

"Okay, what does it look like? What does he look like?"

"He looks like an Indian."

"From India or . . . ?"

"No, from some tribe in America."

Though I was sure he was Native American, I did not know which tribe. He looked at me sternly, seemingly annoyed at being called forth from his stone. Actually it was more like a boulder, part of the promontory of an immense cliff.

"Ask him what his name is."

"Fortune."

"How do you spell it?"

"I don't know. Fortune. Fortune."

The spelling was clear in my head but it seemed a little incongruous to my expectations so I mentally tried out other possibilities such as Forchun and Fourchin. But Fortune insisted on itself.

"Fortune?"

"Mm-hmh."

"Ask him to put his arms around you and give you a big hug and you give him a big hug."

Somehow I could tell that hugging was clearly out of character for Fortune. However, he acquiesced with dignity. He still seemed perturbed at being pulled out of his stone, but his sternness was tempered with kindness.

"How does it feel?

"Nice."

"Ask him if he is going to be your friend and available to you to help you in the future."

"Yes. He says all the time . . . all the time."

"And that you will be able to go to talk to him in your mind and get help and advice when you need it?"

"Mm-hmh."

"And learn how to talk to him and he to talk to you?"

"Yes."

"Good. Ask him what other lifetimes we should examine."

"Just before the one I'm in now."

"All right. We will do that the next time. Ask him what your real mission is in the rest of this lifetime."

"He says I won't know that yet. I will know it."

"I see. 'Cause next time when we get together we will also go up and see him. Ask him if he will be happy to see us."

"Yes, of course."

"I see. Ask him if he has any advice for you at this time that will help you until we can work things out."

"He says what I used to tell the others."

"Huh?"

"He says not to worry."

I laughed. Fortune's using of the same phrase "not to worry," the same one I had used as the psychic woman in Mexico, struck me as funny. His allusion to my own advice seemed like gentle teasing, an overture of friendship, unless, of course, all of this was just my own imagination.

"Do you think you're going to have a good

relationship with him?"

"Yeah."

"Excellent. And now that you have met him, it's going to be so wonderful because you'll be able to get advice and help from him at any time, won't you?"

"Mm-hmh."

"Good. Anything else or should we bring you out of this session?"

"I think that's all."

"All right. We've accomplished quite a bit, haven't we? We're going to let go of all this. You will remain in a very deep, relaxed, peaceful, hypnotic sleep but on the count of three you will be back in the present time here. Now as an absolute command, you will remember every single detail of everything you have perceived while examining this prior incarnation but on the count of three, you will be back in the present time feeling wonderful. One . . . two . . . three . . . All right."

I "woke up" feeling very strange. Though I hadn't been asleep in the normal sense, I had definitely been in something other than my usual waking mode of consciousness. The hypnotic state did feel similar to sleep. But to equate the two is to misrepresent the unique experience of hypnosis. For although I was not totally in my normal waking mode of consciousness, it remained there on the sidelines as what I call my "present mind," continually monitoring all I perceived and felt.

In a way it was like taking a long automobile ride. My past-life mind and my present-life mind were occupants of the car and they took turns driving. My view of the scenery depended on which mind had control of the vehicle at any given moment, and some of these changes were abrupt. For example, when I was completely involved in the past life, if Tom instructed me to move forward, my focus would suddenly shift back to the present life.

It also felt like watching a movie, except that the past life was more real and alive than any movie I had seen. Not only was I watching this movie, I was in it at the same time—hearing, smelling, touching and tasting, as well as seeing. I was extremely absorbed in each sequence and totally invested in the outcome. How could I not be, considering that this was my whole lifetime, or at least the major portion of it, compressed into a mere hour or two in present time?

At the end of this emotional roller coaster ride, it was no wonder I needed some time to unwind and catch my breath. Tom, sensitive to my situation, let me take all the time I needed to feel comfortable in my present space and time again.

When I could finally speak, my first question was, "I'm just making it all up, right?"

"No, you're not," Tom assured me, but I didn't quite believe him. It was easier to believe I was making it up.

"Is this a usual response?" I asked him. "Do most people react this way the first time?"

"Yes, it is very usual, but then eventually most people do come to accept it as real," Tom said. I had to accept the genuineness of the emotions I had felt as Rita. "Yes, well, I accept it as real, a certain kind of real, but is it really a past life? Did it all really happen? And is it really my own past life, not someone else's past life that I just somehow bumped in to?"

Tom warned me that a common reaction after having tapped into a past life through hypnosis is to find oneself becoming more psychic. Psychic occurrences often start popping up. This made sense to me as it had been my experience that when one opens up to a greater reality in any one way, it then makes itself known to you in other, sometimes unexpected, ways as well. It also occurred to me that, having discovered another life of mine where I actually was a psychic, something in me from that life might reemerge in the present life. I watched for this reaction in myself and was curious as to how it might manifest but didn't notice any sign of heightened psychic activity.

However, my so-called normal life over the next few days was far from normal. I couldn't help thinking about the past-life session and its implications. My mind was so occupied with making meaning of it all that I thought I might go crazy. I felt spacey and confused and clung to the physical details and demands of my daily routine to balance the intense metaphysical energies that had been set loose in me. It was much easier to get up, get dressed, make breakfast as usual and get my son off to school and me to work than to mull over whether I lived before and, if I had, whether it was that life as Rita.

From time to time, waves of anxiety would engulf me—anxiety about my own mental state. Had I taken on too much? Could I handle what I was getting myself into? What did it all mean? I longed for some life-jacket of truth in the raging sea of my confusion.

Tom had said to call if I needed to, so I did. He reassured me that it sometimes took time to integrate the information. "Integrating information." Was that all I was doing? It sounded so dry and mechanical. In spite of Tom's attempts to reassure me, I still felt very shaky.

Some days later I discussed the past-life session with a close group of women friends, one of whom was a psychologist. She asked me if it really mattered whether I experienced a past life or not. She suggested my subconscious had manufactured these scenarios to match my conscious life, much as dreams in sleep often mirror one's waking life. So, of course, they would be relevant to my present life's experiences. She suggested that even though they might be complete fantasies, they could still be meaningful. Perhaps the source of the information really didn't matter as much as the content itself.

I was willing to try on this idea . . . at least for a while. But soon I found myself back at the reference section of the library trying to verify the details of the past life. I looked through modern maps for the old town, Guahaca or Huahaca or Guahuaca, that I had supposedly lived near, seeking verification that I wasn't making all this up. And even if it didn't prove that it was my past life, at least it might prove to be somebody's past life. My first cursory attempts at research turned up nothing conclusive. I was discouraged. I told myself that towns can change their names or die altogether so that even if I couldn't find it on a modern map of Mexico, a town by that name could have existed there in the 1700s. But the spelling of the town could take several forms because Rita of the past life was not educated and probably couldn't spell well and over hundreds of years the actual spelling could have changed from one mapmaker to another. Was it Oaxaca?

I felt torn between looking further and giving up while I still had some room for belief. I was afraid that if I investigated too thoroughly, it might all prove to be phony. Perhaps it was better after all just to focus on what I could learn rather than what I could prove. As for the content, it definitely had meaning for me. During my session itself, my present mind was constantly making connections from past to present, some links being more obvious than others.

What was clear was that my brother in that life ran and fell off a cliff and was killed when I was supposed to be watching out for him. The guilt and recrimination that followed colored the rest of that life and carried over into this one. In my present life as a preschool teacher of four-year-olds like my past-life brother, I have always had, strangely, somewhat more concern about the well-being of the boys than the girls. Other teachers noticed similar tendencies in themselves too, but it bothered me to the extent that, for the sake of professional conduct and personal peace of mind, I consciously balanced the concentration on the boys with deliberate and equal attention to the girls.

However, there emerged a bigger issue. In my work

as a preschool teacher, I had always had a feeling, a fearful feeling, that something bad might happen to one of the children in my care, not because of anything I might do but rather because of something I might not do. In spite of complimentary reports on my teaching from other teachers, administrators, parents, and the children themselves, I doubted my own ability. Of course, my conscientiousness may have been overcompensating for these left-over feelings of failure. The death of my past-life brother while under my care coupled with my past-life mother's subsequent decline and death weighed too heavily on my psyche. This time around, my great desire to teach and care for children was accompanied by an equally strong feeling that I was unable to do the job well.

Being off with my first boyfriend, as I saw it, had allowed for my brother's demise. When the calamity occurred, I was enjoying myself instead of doing my duty. This too has had a carryover into the current lifetime so far. I have strongly put duty before pleasure and, those few times I haven't, I have managed to make myself feel quite guilty about it.

Perhaps the most distressing thing that happened directly in that lifetime was that, once I finally was able to marry and start a family of my own, the baby was born dead. To make matters worse, I couldn't bear any more children after that. To my way of thinking as Rita, this was obvious retribution for my being happily in love and married to the man I loved when I should have been suffering forever for my earlier mistake. The message came through loud and clear that I was not deserving of a happy life. The anguish of bearing a stillborn baby might explain why in my present lifetime I also became a teacher of prepared childbirth. Without really examining any possible reason for it at the time, I was drawn to helping women bear happy, healthy children through the easiest, most joyful deliveries possible. Emotionally involved in the work, I especially put a lot of effort into easing the fears of the pregnant women who came to my classes.

Another connection between the past and present lives was that, at the end of the past life, I became a psychic. People would come to me for "readings" from the stars. Although I did not know astrology then, my inspiration came by looking through the stars. In my present lifetime, I have studied astrology and worked as a certified astrologer, people coming to me again for what wisdom the stars might impart.

Some of these connections between my past and present life were immediately obvious, others surfaced over weeks and months. Still others would become apparent with time. But one thing was clear: this one session had a most positive result. The overall effect has been freeing, as if someone had opened a door to say, "There is more outside this cramped little room you've been in. You may go out if you like."

It so happened that a neurosurgeon friend of mine was in town shortly after I did this first past-life session. I knew that he was not only well-trained and experienced on the physical level of his profession, but well-read on metaphysical issues as well. I took the opportunity of his visit to ask him about his thoughts on the past life. He read the transcription of the first session and was very interested in it. Later, in correspondence, he revealed a caution about delving into this area. His understanding was that a past-life re-experienced through hypnosis could well be a reading of some of the material laid down in the akasa or Akashic records, the Almighty Cosmic Library in the Sky, as I call it. He said the ability to tap into these records depends on a person's refinement of mental ability, which in turn depends on a high stage of spiritual growth. Given such development and ability to concentrate, a person might be able to tap into the section of the records that pertained to him or her, and the hypnotist could serve as a guide.

Then too, he said, there was a certain element of balance involved in the depth of mind reached through hypnosis. Too light and you get nothing; too deep and you can't retrieve it to make use of it in the present mode. He also pointed out the delicate responsibility of the hypnotist towards the client and the telepathic link that can develop between hypnotist and client. I had already experienced telepathy with Tom. He often seemed to be able to see and feel what I was seeing and feeling in the past life. Sometimes his questions seemed leading but his being on the same wavelength, so to speak, turned out to be more of an asset than a liability. It served to keep things moving in a productive way.

Tom confirmed that, depending on the rapport with any particular person, he did pick up information telepathically to varying degrees. The neurosurgeon's main point was that past-life probes had their uses and their limitations. One had to proceed with great caution and with recognition of the fact that one's own spiritual growth was far more important. His opinion reminded me of my own understanding of the issue, an issue I consider rather important.

I describe this issue as the difference between the psychic and the spiritual. The spiritual relates to the growth and evolution of the soul. It refers to the most meaningful lessons of life, which are not always apparent. The psychic has to do with tools to use or signals to draw one's attention to the deeper spiritual issues. For example, if a person were to receive by some unusual means a message about one's life from someone at a physical distance or perhaps even dead, the conveyance of the message is psychic, whereas how one puts that message to work in his or her life is their spiritual work.

I would describe one's spiritual life as a path that one journeys. Along the way are occasional signposts for direction. Some of the signposts can be very distracting, especially if they lie beyond the borders of one's familiar sense of order or if they appear suddenly or dramatically. A person can get distracted by the glitz and glamour of the psychic sideshow and end up neglecting the main event.

I could see that this was a temptation for me in terms of the past-life work. I was so amazed by how it worked, as if it were some sort of magic trick. I could easily become entranced with the marvelous experiences and forget that I could be learning something from it all. I had made some superficial connections between the past life and my present one but sensed there was more to it than that.

Aside from the past life itself, the session included the meeting with Fortune, the spirit guide or "master," as Tom called him. This whole sequence was strangely different from the rest of the session. The past life itself was rich with vivid, sensorial experience. I felt the heat of the sun, the relief of cool shade, smelled the wine and the sweat of the dancers, heard the music in the church. By contrast, after the death in that life, there was a marked lack of concreteness. Sensation was abstracted, nebulous. I couldn't really touch, hear, smell or see in the same way that I could during the life. And this made it difficult to answer the questions Tom put to me, especially about description. I was being asked to extricate something palpable from what was no more solid than fog. "Stone" was how I could best describe the feeling of solidity of the land formation from which Fortune emerged. But it wasn't real stone or earth. Rather it was the essence or the idea of it.

It was a struggle to call forth from this earth-ness or stone-ness the figure that eventually emerged. And yet he did appear, dressed lightly in leathers and feathers and embodying austerity and wisdom. I sensed that he was willing to be there, to be of help and guidance but reluctantly so as if he were saying, "Okay, you pulled me out and here I am for you, if you are willing to work at this too."

Feeling like an uninvolved middleman, I relayed

the questions and answers between Tom and Fortune. I didn't quite fathom what was going on and participated only minimally. In the days following the session, I focused my attention on the past life itself and let the part about Fortune rest. I had no idea at the time that Fortune would become so important.

Chapter Three
As Susan in England

While trying to sort out the meaning of the past-life session, I passed along to my friend Andrew not only the contact information for Tom Thomason, but I also related the details of the session to him. He was fascinated and made an appointment for himself for when his busy work schedule permitted some time off. Meanwhile, my own curiosity compelled me to continue exploring this strange new thing.

I made another appointment with Tom, following Fortune's suggestion, to look at the past life immediately preceding my present one. Now that I knew a bit more about the hypnosis routine, I was less nervous about that part of it. The doubts I had about whether I could be hypnotized were greatly diminished. In fact, Tom said that in his years of work he had noticed that people could usually be hypnotized more quickly and deeply with each subsequent session. He also included a suggestion to this effect in the induction process.

As for the whole idea of past lives and spirit guides and the premise on which we were operating, I was still doubtful. When I saw Tom, we talked briefly about this and my other reactions to the first session. He was concerned about my feeling confused and said we could wait before going further but I was ready to do more. I wanted confirmation of the reality of these other "worlds" and thought that immersing myself in another past life might very well provide that. And so we began again.

Tom used the same induction technique as before, offering suggestions for deeper relaxation as well as helpful images ending with a time tunnel out of which I emerged into the past life.

"You are now there. You are fifteen years of age in the lifetime just prior to your present incarnation. I want you to take a look around and tell me: Where are you? Indoors or out-of-doors?"

I was standing outside a row of houses attached to each other, each with a small front yard surrounded by a low fence of iron grillwork and tall steps to the front door. The neighborhood appeared to be upper class.

"Are you male or female?"

"Female."

"How are you dressed?"

"I have a grey dress on. Striped, comes to my knees, low waist."

"Is it an inexpensive dress or a very nice one?"

"Actually, it's a rather nice one."

"Do you have shoes on?"

"Yes, black ones."

"And stockings?"

"Long socks.

They were white knee socks.

"Do you have a ribbon in your hair or do you have a little hat on?"

"I have a little ribbon . . . black ribbon . . . red hair . . . curly."

"Are you a very pretty girl?"

"Mmm . . . kind of."

I was laughing at Tom's asking if I had a little hat on because I certainly did wear hats, and little ones at that, but at the moment there was no special occasion for wearing one. Still, the image of those little hats on my big head of curly red hair was somehow amusing to my present mind.

As for being pretty, people had said I was, and the red hair always got attention. I was also a bit spoiled, being an only child, but my upbringing included learning to be modest about one's looks, so my "yes" to the question of whether I was pretty was subdued.

"What country are you living in?"

"England."

"And what is the year?"

"18 . . . something . . ."

"Think hard."

Thinking "hard" didn't help. Then I remembered Tom saying before just to say whatever came to mind. That seemed less forceful, more promising.

"1858."

"Uh-huh. Do you live with your parents?"

"Yes."

"And you're out in the country now?"

"I'm not in the country."

"You're just outside."

"Yes, on the street."

"Do you have brothers and sisters?"

"No."

"What is your name?"

"Susan."

"And do you live with your mother and father?"

"Yes."

"What's their name?"

"Bentley."

"Mm-hmh."

"Martha."

"What's their last name, their surname?"

"Cook."

"Where do you live in England?"

"London."

"What do you do? Do you go to school?"

"Yes, with other girls."

"Is your family fairly wealthy?"

"Yes."

"What does your father do?"

"He's a businessman."

"What kind of business does he do?"

"He imports, exports."

"Do you travel at all with him?"

"No."

"Does he travel much?"

"Mm-hmh."

"Would you like to travel with him?"

"Yeah. He complains about the travel so . . . I don't ask."

"Is it just that he doesn't want to be away from his family, or because it's unpleasant?"

"He complains about where he goes."

"Are you a happy child?"

"Yes."

I didn't like being called a child. I thought of myself as more grown-up than that!

"How old are you?"

"I'm fifteen."

"Do you have any boyfriends?"

"No."

And I certainly wouldn't have admitted it if I did, perhaps because I was a bit uncertain about how I did feel about boys, and perhaps because I wasn't supposed to have boyfriends. Nonetheless, I was fascinated by male energy. The very unfamiliarity of it spelled adventure. My secure world of family and girls' school was beginning to be all too familiar and predictable.

"Are you a shy girl or a very aggressive little redhead?"

"Sometimes I'm a little frisky."

"Do you get in trouble with your mother once in a while?"

"Not so much with my mother, but at school."

"Ah. Are you a pretty good student . . . when you aren't acting up?"

"Yes." I laughed at what Tom said.

"Have any special friends?"

"I have some girlfriends at school."

"What do you do when you aren't in school? Do you have any hobbies?"

"Sometimes I go to a park with my friends from school."

"Mm-hmh."

"We have big hoops and we race them in the park."

Bloody terrors we were! We would take sticks and race the hoops down the walkways, and when several of us did it together, we often frightened other people. We were really a bit too old for the game by now but I felt very powerful in that group. Perhaps on my own I wouldn't have done it, or at least not as wildly.

"Are you a tall girl, fat or slim, or what?"

"Normal."

"Mm-hmh."

"Kind of small . . . maybe."

"Anything else you'd like to tell me or shall we move you forward in time a little bit?"

It took me a moment to shift to my present mind. That is, choosing to move forward in the time of the past life was something that could only be done from the perspective of my present life, not within the past life itself.

"All right. Let's move forward to where you are eighteen years of age. On the count of three. One . . . two . . . three. Where are you now?"

"I'm walking down the street outside of the house where we live."

"Mm-hmh."

"And I'm waiting for my father to come home. He's coming back from a trip. He should be coming any time now."

"Do you miss him?"

"Yes. I'm looking forward to seeing him. He goes away a lot and it's nice to see him when he comes back."

"Where has he gone this time?"

"India."

"That takes a long time, doesn't it?"

"Yeah, he's been gone . . . months."

"How do you and your mother get along?"

"Fine."

"Are you through school now?"

"Yeah, it's just finished. I'm not quite sure what's going to happen next."

"Have you met any boys that you go out with or that you're interested in?"

"No, not really. My mother has some friends that have sons about my age. They come to the house sometimes but they're not boyfriends."

"What would you like to do? Would you like to work with your father in the business?"

"I don't think so. I want to do something on my own."

"All right. Anything else you'd like to tell me or shall we move forward in time a couple of years to see what happens to you?"

"Well, I kind of want to hear about India from my dad."

"All right. Let's move forward just in time to where your dad is home and you're getting a chance to find out what happened to him there. One . . . two . . . three. You're now with your dad."

"There are a lot of other people. I can't talk to him now. They're having a party for him coming back."

"How does he look?"

"Great."

"Was it a successful trip as far as you know?"

"Yes. He says there are a lot of things happening in India and everybody should pay attention there now."

"Mm-hmh!"

"But I want to see what he looks like when he's in India. I asked him if he'd wear the clothes that he wears there but he said he doesn't bring them back."

"That was a disappointment, wasn't it?"

"Well, you know, I didn't really expect it. It's just that he tells these stories and I like to picture him doing it so I . . . I'd like to see him."

"Is your father a very handsome man?"

"Yes."

"Is he very popular with the ladies?"

"Yes."

Here Tom was a bit ahead of me again. My father was not only good-looking but very charming. Although it always seemed to take a little time for him to switch back to home life after being away, once he did so he was confidently on top of any situation whether business or social.

It was his other life traveling that I was curious about. He often told stories but they were always in the impersonal tone of a public statement. I think my interest in his wearing his other clothes was fostered by desire to see if that would bring out his personal feelings about his other, and to my mind more adventurous, life.

"Is he very popular with your mother?"

"Yes, they're playful, especially right now. My mother is really glad to see him."

"It's been a long dry spell, hasn't it?"

I understood this question to have a sexual connotation and I appreciated that I was thought old enough to comprehend the meaning without having it spelled out as such. It was the custom to refer to anything sexual obliquely.

"All right. Let's move forward just a few days to where the party's over and you have a chance to talk to your dad. What did you find out that was important to you?"

"He said that it's really good I studied history in school."

The role of women was becoming a social issue but it had been a personal issue with me for some time. My father and mother allowed me to do much more than many other girls were allowed then. Both of them were quite progressive in their ideas but they were also living in a society that frowned on too much independence in women. They had to cater to that as well. Certainly, I could be very outspoken. For the sake of decorum, my mother was interested in curbing my outspoken tendency, a trait that she herself shared to a milder degree. My father was convinced that my boisterous energy just needed channeling in some useful direction.

"He says I should pay attention to what goes on in the world."

"Does that interest you?"

"It's more alive than what happened before but . . ."

"Mm-hmh."

"He says pay attention to any kind of history, any

kind of history."

"'Cause that's the record of the world, isn't it?"

"Mm-hmh."

"Are you happy now that you have had a chance to talk to him?"

"Yeah, except that I'm still not quite sure what to do."

"All right. On the count of three, let's move forward a year to where you're nineteen and see what's happened. One . . . two . . . three. Where are you now?"

"I am working in the office of one of my father's friends. He's a lawyer. I greet people when they come in to see the lawyer and give them tea if they need to wait. It's kind of boring but it's all right."

"Have you met any interesting people?"

"Oh, yeah. A lot of people come through. Well, I don't know if they're that interesting. I don't get to talk to them for very long before Mr. Cranshaw is ready to see them."

"Mm-hmh. What do you do with your spare time?"

"I occasionally get together with some friends of mine from school. We go to one house or another house and sometimes if it's nice out we go for a picnic in the country, maybe six or eight of us."

"All girls, or girls and boys?"

"Girls and boys!"

My present mind noted the "six or eight," which sounded like an arrangement by couples. In fact we did seem to pair off, but not formally. There were certain liaisons that we made allowances for in our plans and activities but having it be so loose and unstated permitted changes in these friendships without too much embarrassment. Also, the group provided the function of a chaperone, whereas going out in twos or even by fours unchaperoned was not encouraged.

"Have you met anyone special?"

"Well . . . not special like that . . . 'cept—"

"Hmm?"

"I was just thinking about the last time we went out in the country. There was this lake and I was showing off a little bit and fell in." I started laughing at this.

"Uh-oh. What did your mother say when you got home?"

"She wasn't too happy about it, but I think it was 'cause she knew I was probably doing something a little silly. She's a lot like me though so she has a hard time being mad."

"She recognizes a lot of herself in you?"

"Oh yeah. She said once it's because we both have red hair."

Before this session was underway, I had asked Tom if it would be possible to find certain people from my present life in a past life. He had said it was possible and took down the names of the people I had in mind. But he said that certain people come and go over many lives so a person might not appear in the particular past life being reexamined.

"Do any of the following names from your present lifetime have any meaning in this incarnation—Robbie Winston, Theodore Olson, Clark Carter, Andrew

Petrovski?"

Now when Tom asked, the names sounded ridiculously foreign to me. I was so immersed in the past life that it took me a moment to pull out of it enough to remember who the people were at all. The four names were of four men I knew in different ways in my present lifetime. Robbie Winston was someone with whom I had a casual, friendly, almost flirty relationship. My relationship with Theodore Olson was a more serious personal relationship, with a strong pull between us from the very beginning. We were close for several years until the relationship seemed to play out and end. Clark Carter was someone I worked with. We also shared a love of music and occasionally played music together outside of work hours. As for Andrew Petrovski, he was the friend who had originally asked about past-life work and so was the one most directly responsible for starting me on the past-life adventures. When Tom asked about these four at this point, there seemed to be no obvious connections.

"Not that I know of."

"Mm-hmh. At least not yet. Okay. You're nineteen years of age now. Let's move forward to where you're twenty. One . . . two . . . three. Still working in the same office?"

"I'm not there much of the time. I've been reading on the history of London. My dad says pay attention to history. I've been doing that. And sometimes when the people come to see the lawyer, I show them around a bit of London, point out all the historical places, where everything is, you know, show them old houses and the new houses and where things happened."

"Give them a quick history of London? That's rather unusual for a girl back in that time, isn't it?"

"Well, yeah, it is a little bit, I think."

It was the result of a talk between my father, Mr. Cranshaw, and myself that this "tour guide" idea came up—extended duty as receptionist for people coming into London from out of town. My mother was hesitant about the idea so it was suggested that she might accompany me. On those occasions, we made visits to her friends' houses where our guests were received as well.

"How do you go? In a carriage?"

"Sometimes. It depends, you know. Mr. Cranshaw has a carriage that he shares with somebody but if the horses are around and the carriage is free and also Gus, the driver, then we get to go in the carriage, which is nice."

"Mm-hmh."

"But sometimes we walk. Then we can't go so far. They get tired or it gets a little muddy on the dress."

"Your dresses reach all the way to the ground?"

"Mm-hmh. I don't wear short ones anymore."

When I began working, I began wearing women's clothes rather than school girl's outfits. My adult mode of dress was a facet of seeing myself as grown-up as was using whatever slang I could get away with it. I'm guessing that the actual words were different but in the sessions they came across as "you know" and "yeah," the modern equivalents of what would have been slang then.

"All right. Letting go of all of this, without any

stress or strain, move forward to when you're twenty-three years of age, unless something of importance has happened. One . . . two . . . three. Where are you now?"

"I'm visiting my mother in the hospital. She's had some sort of operation, but she's going to be fine."

"Mm-hmh!"

"She says she's too strong and stubborn to die so I shouldn't worry. Besides, she has to stick around to keep me in line."

Tom laughed.

"Sounds as though you and your mother have a close relationship. How about you and your dad? Are you getting along well too?"

"Yeah. My dad says that I might be able to go with him next time he takes a trip."

"Wonderful! You don't have any special boyfriends then, or nobody of interest?"

"Well, there is this guy named Martin that's been working with my dad. On the next trip, they might go back to India but my dad says it's not a good idea to take a woman there now. Maybe I'll get to go anyway if Martin doesn't go. So I'm kind of hoping he doesn't. But Martin is my friend so . . ."

Although Martin actually wanted to be a little more than just a friend, he kept a social distance. He was concerned about getting involved with the boss's daughter even though I think he secretly hoped it would turn out that way. As for me, I liked him well enough, but if it came down to a choice between the two of us for going on the trip, I didn't want to get emotionally involved with him if either one of us were to go off. So we were just friends.

"I see. And a very good friend?"

"Well, kind of. He tries to be serious."

"And that drives you crazy, doesn't it?"

"Well, not really, but sometimes he's so stiff."

"Mm-hmh. What do you want him to do?"

"Loosen up."

"Throw his arms around you and . . ."

"Actually he should just get good and drunk once."

"Have you told him this?"

"Yeah, sure."

"Does he drink at all?"

"Oh yeah. It's just that he wants to please my dad 'cause he's been working with him. He's just very careful, so careful."

"Mm-hmh."

"He was with me that day I fell in the lake and he got all red in the face he was so embarrassed. I thought it was funny because I should have been the one to be embarrassed. I mean I looked a mess, but Martin, no . . . he's always . . . just proper."

"Very insecure young boy . . . or young man, I should say."

"He's not that insecure. It's just the way he is."

"Mm-hmh."

"He's just, you know. Anyway he's not sure he wants to go to India. He's afraid he'll get dirty."

I wasn't sure what this fear of getting dirty was about, but Tom moved the story along before my present mind had a chance to sort out possible meanings.

"All right. Shall we move forward in time now and see if you go? On the count of three. One . . . two . . . three. What's happening?"

"I'm twenty-five. We're going to go to India. It's going to be a long trip."

"Mm-hmh."

"My mother doesn't know what to make of it. She says some young ladies just don't know how to be ladies, but I'm going anyway."

"Secretly she'd really like to go with you, wouldn't she?"

"Yeah. She won't admit it but she's real curious. I think she's a bit frightened, too, actually. I'm her one and only daughter and she's pretty proud of me. If I go off to India, who knows what might happen, and after all the stories my dad's told."

I began to feel tightness in my chest but didn't know why.

"I'm twenty-six and I didn't go."

"You didn't go?"

"No. I actually got scared."

"Is your dad still in India?"

"Yeah, he took Martin with him."

"Are you still working at the lawyer's office?"

"Sometimes. There's just so much more happening when my dad is around, more people coming in and so forth. When he's gone, it's kind of dull."

"You still live at home?"

"Yeah, of course."

"Any other boyfriends now that Martin's gone?"

"Yeah, there's George."

"What kind of a joker is George?"

"He is a joker!" I laughed. "He is working for Mr. Cranshaw too and doesn't really like it. He said he'd rather manage a pub and if he could get enough money to have a pub of his own, he'd like to do that. I think he wants us to get married and then I could work in the pub with him. He said I'd be good at it because I enjoy people."

"What do you think of that idea?"

"I don't know. It's kind of adventurous but I don't know, maybe a little seedy."

"It doesn't quite fit into your background, does it?"

"Well, that too, but nobody knows yet anyway. He's told me but he hasn't told anybody else."

"Okay. Shall we move forward a year and see what happens after you're twenty-seven? One . . . two . . . three. Where are you now?"

"Just doing the same stuff. You know, like showing people around when they come. And my dad's still in India with Martin."

"He's been there a long time."

"Yeah, well, there's a lot of stuff going on in India."

"When you say 'a lot of stuff'—"

"Political stuff. It's not really clear whether it's a good idea that he keeps doing his business there. In fact, I'm getting this really tight feeling. I'm afraid something's happened to him or to Martin."

The tightness in my chest came on very strong here,

which worried me.

"All right. Without any strain and no emotion, let's move forward to where you're thirty and tell me what is happening."

"My dad was killed in India."

"During an uprising?"

"Yeah. Martin's come back and . . ." I sighed a long deep sigh.

"Without any emotion now, just simply as an observer."

Had I been less immersed in the emotion of the past life here, I probably would have commented on the term "uprising." This word triggered a sympathetic response in me to whoever was rising up just because the word itself implied pompousness on the part of those who must have been pushing down. However, since my father, or more generally the British, must have been the oppressor, I would probably have had divided loyalties on the issue. As it was, the personal loss overshadowed any such political considerations.

"I wish I'd gone. I wish I'd gone. Maybe I could've helped him." Again I sighed heavily.

"Where was he in India when he was killed?"

"He was in Delhi. Near Delhi."

"How did your mother take it?"

"Oh, gosh, I don't know who's taking it harder, her or me."

"Are you closer to Martin now?"

"No. It's kind of confused. He says maybe if I'd gone instead of him . . . I don't know. He thinks I'm too wild, thinks I want to go just 'cause of all the action there. It's true, but then it's the action that killed my dad."

"How did Martin escape?"

"He wasn't, you know, with my dad. He'd already left."

It was the emotional aftermath of my father's death that brought out the true colors, or at least the worst colors, in Martin and myself. Our pent-up grief, self-recrimination, and anger were let loose at each other in furious shouting matches that destroyed whatever good feeling we had had for each other. He criticized me for being rebellious but fearful, for talking loud but not following through, such as my professing to want to go to India and then backing out. On the other hand, I found it hard to forgive him for "allowing" my father to die in India. I claimed I wouldn't have let it happen. Our political ideas were poles apart as well and I knew I couldn't live with that.

"Okay. Let's move you forward to thirty-one years of age. Where are you and what's happening? Are you still in England?"

"Yeah, but nothing's happening. It's like a dead city."

"Are you still working at the lawyer's office?"

"I go by there occasionally but it's mostly for old times' sake. My mom isn't doing too well. She's like an old lady now. She always wears black, wants me to wear black. I think she's still mourning my father."

"Mm-hmh."

"I feel kind of guilty about it but still . . . he's dead."

"It was supposed to happen. There was nothing you

could do about it."

"I don't know. Somehow I feel I could have done something. I could have, you know."

"Influenced him not to take so many chances?"

"Well, I might have taken the same chances. That's the thing."

"Mm-hmh."

"But if I'd just been with him . . . I don't know."

"You can't accept the responsibility for his life. Shall we move forward now to where you're thirty-five and see what is happening?"

"I want to see if my mom is going to be all right. I want to find somebody to take care of her. I just can't do it all the time. I mean I've got my own life."

"She's tying you down and not allowing you to live?"

"Yeah. I mean I'm not dead. She can be dead if she wants to be but . . ."

"All right. You're thirty-one years of age now. Let's move forward to where you've got somebody to take care of your mother. On the count of three, without any stress or strain . . . "

"I'm thirty-two and uh . . . well, Martin's a lost cause. But George is finally doing some things. We're going to India."

"Have you got somebody to take care of your mother?"

"Yeah, her sister's gonna come over."

"Excellent."

"They're a bunch of old fuddy-duddies. They have black umbrellas, black everything, black clothes, black stockings. The whole house seems black now. Even my aunt says she ought to liven up. My mother's just killing herself. I've gotta get out!"

"All right. Let's move forward now to where you and George are in India. On the count of three, tell me how old you are, where you are and if you had a good trip . . ."

"I'm thirty-four." And then very quietly, I said, "We didn't make it to India."

"Where did you go?"

"We got to Holland. Not very far, but at least it's out of the dead house."

"What are you doing there?"

"He's got a pub. It's an English pub in Amsterdam."

"I see. And are you the barmaid?"

"I'm not the barmaid. I help run the place."

"Are you the hostess then?"

"I am the manager."

I was very particular about the choice of words because I was self-conscious about being anything as lowly as a barmaid, given both my background and my dreams of adventure and ambition.

"I see. Do you buy the supplies, see that employees are hired and paid and the like?"

"Actually, I'm not even there that much." For some reason, I giggled. "Now I'm learning all about the history of Amsterdam."

"Are you married?"

"Oh yeah. We have a baby girl."

"What's her name?"

"Josie."

"For Josephine?"

"It has nothing to do with her real name, but it's about as strong a name as you can get and still have it sound like she's a girl."

"Is she like you?"

"She's got red hair like me."

Red hair was important to me as an indication of high-spirited character. I was pleased my daughter resembled my mother and myself in that respect.

"And does she keep you on the run?"

"I take her with me everywhere I go."

"How do you and George get along? Is he a good husband?"

"Yeah. He says I'm a pretty lively lady and sometimes calls me Fireball."

Having left England and also working in a pub gave me leeway to be the feisty, temperamental person that I was. There were lots of arguments with George but it provided for some sparks of the best kind in bed, although I had enough manners not to say as much. It seems my temperament needed some sort of sparring partner. George wasn't quite up to it and became increasingly less so as he got older. This was a source of frustration for me as well as my not being able to go off and see the world. It would have been a life of quiet desperation except for that fact that I was far from quiet. Perhaps it could be called a life of noisy desperation!

"All right. On the count of three, I want you to move forward to where you're thirty-seven years of age. One . . . two . . . three. Where are you now?"

"Down by the docks."

"In Amsterdam?"

"Yeah."

"Why? Do you want to travel some more?"

"Yeah. I've been trying to tell George we ought to go."

"Where do you want to go?"

"Anywhere. Just somewhere . . . take Josie and go."

"Let's move forward in time to where you take Josie, and George, if he wants to go, and see where you arrive at. Where are you now?"

"Nowhere. I have another baby, a little boy, without going anywhere."

"Are you unhappy?"

"Not really, but I wonder what it's like somewhere else."

"What's the baby's name?"

"John."

"Is he a redhead too?"

"Kind of. He's more like his dad."

"Mm-hmh."

"I guess George is getting like Martin. He's getting a little . . ."

"Formal?"

"Not formal, really, but staid, unadventurous. He likes the pub, all the regulars that come in, and he's getting so English. I thought he wanted to get away too, but he doesn't want to do anything, doesn't want to go anywhere." I whispered, but strongly, "I'd like to leave the kids with him and just get on a ship—and go!"

This was a sentiment that would not have aroused much public support then. In fact, it seems rather like a private confession, thus the whispered but still emphatic tone.

"All right. Let's move forward to when you're forty years of age and see what happens. One . . . two . . . three. Are you still in Amsterdam?"

"Yup."

"Another child?"

"No, just got the two."

"You sound frustrated."

"Well, what I'm doing is writing. If I can't go somewhere, I'm going to write about it. I talk to everybody that gets off the boats and they tell me about where they've been and I write it down."

"What is the most fascinating place for you? India? Africa? Europe? America?"

"Indonesia."

"Mm-hmh."

"You asked about somebody . . ."

"Robbie Winston? Theodore Olson? Carter? Andrew Petrovski?"

These were the same four names of people in my present life that Tom asked about earlier in the session. I was curious as to whether I had had a past-life connection with any of them.

"Andrew Petrovski. Yeah. He's on the ships, one of the guys that tell me about a lot of places."

"Is he a sailor or an officer on the ships, or what?"

"He's not anything official. He's—"

"A deckhand?"

"Not officially even that," I whispered. "He stowed away on the last one."

"Uh-huh!"

"He was just lucky that he got to where he was going and came back in one piece. I've heard of other people that didn't have that luck."

"Is he your friend?"

"He tells me a lot about Indonesia. Indo-nee-sia. He doesn't call it that."

"What does he call it?"

"I guess he's never called it anything. He just tells about it."

"Is he a good friend of yours?"

"Well, he knows I want to travel. He knows I'm writing everything down so he tries to tell me but, you know, he's kind of here today, gone tomorrow."

"Mm-hmh."

"He's trying to get on another ship. I told him he should be more careful. He might not make it back next time. Sometimes they actually dump people overboard. I can't believe it. I mean, that's second-hand, but I believe it."

I was thinking in my present mind that there was so much coincidence between the past life and present life of this person, Andrew, whom I had asked about that I didn't trust the past life story. I figured, again, that I had just made it up.

No name emerged for this past-life adventurous deckhand but one parallel with Andrew Petrovski in my present life was remarkable. Andrew Petrovski, who was older than myself, was born in Europe, traveled to live in the United States, but had a strong business connection with Indonesia. I did not know Andrew Petrovski when he was in a young, perhaps more reckless, period of his present life. But the fact that even now he was curious enough to pursue past lives showed a similar venturesome spirit. And even though I didn't fully trust the past-life material, something did ring true between this supposed past-life version of Andrew and what I knew of his present life.

"All right. Let's move forward to when you're forty-five, unless something of importance happens and you make a trip. One . . . two . . . three. Where are you now?"

"Back in England."

"With George?"

"Yeah, we all came back. My mother died. I feel bad about that 'cause I wasn't there when it happened."

"She lived a long time though, didn't she?"

"It was as if she were in a museum ever since my dad died."

"Are you going to stay in England?"

"I hope not, but George wants to. I want to go back to Amsterdam. Anywhere!"

"All right. Shall we move forward in time to where you're fifty years of age and see if you go someplace? On the count of three. One . . . two . . . three. Where are you now?"

"George had his way. We're in England and he's got a pub. It's not actually his. He's got a partner. He had it better in Amsterdam. I'm there now just some of the time or home with the kids."

"Mm-hmh."

"Josie's so cute. God, she's cute, real cute."

"Is she a little stinker like you were?"

"She's probably going to have an easier time."

Social freedom for women was increasing. If she were the least bit spunky, it would be easier for her than it had been for me to make her own way. I could see a bit of change from my mother's time to mine. My parents, especially my father, were more progressive than the norm in allowing for women's independence. However, I don't think I was independent in the ways that my father had in mind. He thought I might follow in his footsteps professionally but all my energy tended to be loud and willful rather than ambitious in any disciplined way.

"Josie doesn't take after her mother?"

"No, she's more like her dad. I just thought with her red hair and all . . . But she's quiet. I keep wanting her to kind of . . . oh, I don't know."

"Show a little more spunk?"

"Yeah. She's a nice girl though. I should be happy but I have a sneaky feeling that if she were just a little more lively, when she grew up I could tag along with her somewhere."

Upon hearing my past self say this, my present mind took to pitying Josie for this impending imposition on her life by a frustrated mother.

"You're fifty years of age now. What kind of shape are you in? Good physical condition?"

"Oh, yeah. Still slim and trim."

"How's George? Is he getting a little heavy now?"

"He's got a little bit of a beer tummy, but no big deal."

"Still a good lover?"

"Mm-hmh."

"Do you enjoy making love?"

"Yeah, but I'm restless, got this long dissatisfaction with just about everything else."

"Have you ever had any other lover besides George?"

"Close but not quite. I mean you gotta draw the line somewhere."

Geez, this guy is nosey, thought my past-life self. I didn't like these personal questions at all, but at least he pressed the issue politely.

"Okay. Let's move forward to where you're fifty-five and see what's happening. Is that all right with you?"

"Fifty-five?"

"Mm-hmh. On the count of three."

"No-o-o. Fifty-two."

"All right. Fifty-two. What's happening?"

"We're not in London, but living on a farm that used to belong to my aunt."

"Mm-hmh."

"Farm life is not for me. It's not much of a farm anyway and such a long way off from London, where everything's going on."

"Is George happy with it?"

"Oh, yeah. He's just, you know, all of a sudden, he's Old Farmer George. He should have been doing this a long time ago."

"Children are in good shape?"

"Fine."

"All right. Let's move forward to where you're sixty and . . ."

"I don't even want to talk about this life."

Though I had obviously been talking about the life for quite some time already, my statement came from a point of sufficient age to be able to look back over my life and evaluate it. Perhaps it was because I sensed the life coming to its completion that I could now afford to make a judgment and, having found it wanting and without much time left to make amends, was ready to give up on it.

"Let's try to take it out to the end here, and move forward to where you're sixty, if you're still alive."

"I can't get to sixty."

"Then let's move forward to the last day of your life in this incarnation. Now as an absolute command, you will feel no pain or emotion. You'll experience this situation objectively and only as an observer. One . . . two . . . three. How old are you now?"

I said very quietly, "Fifty-eight."

"Are you still on the farm?"

Mouthing the words but with no sound coming out, I tried to say, "I can't talk."

"What's the matter? Are you very ill?"

Still mouthing the words with barely a sound, "I can't talk."

"You can't talk? I want you to disregard the fact

that you're so ill. On the count of three, without pain or emotion, I want you to leave your physical body and cross over into spirit and find yourself in spirit just a few moments after experiencing your physical death in the incarnation we're now examining. One . . . two . . . three. You're now in the spirit world. Do you feel any better?"

"How stupid! What a crazy way to die!"

"What happened? How did you die?"

"Fell into the river."

"And drowned?"

"No, they got me out but I didn't live very long."

"I see. Were you still on the farm then?"

"No. We'd gone to London for a trip. I just didn't want to go back to the farm so George and I had a big argument. We were walking by the side of the river and we argued. It was quite a scene." I sighed. "Of course, that's what I was doing all the time, making one scene after another. He just hit me."

"And knocked you into the river?"

"Right into the river!"

"Was George anybody that you know in this present incarnation?"

"No."

"He has no role in this present life?"

"No."

When I was taken to the last day of that life, I was in a hospital in a coma. The river I had fallen into was bordered by a steep stone embankment. On the top of it there was a walkway, which is where the argument took place. I didn't know how to swim, and because it was so far down to the water, saving me was rather difficult. I recalled that, as a young woman and as a result of the same impudence, I had fallen into a lake, an incident which, in literary terms, would be called a foreshadowing of my later demise.

At this point I could already begin to see a few connections between the past life and my present life. I suppose I have always been something of an Anglophile. I have lived in London, Bristol, and the Midlands of England in my present life. And it is curious that the cause of death in that life—drowning—may have been the unconscious impetus for learning to swim in this present life. More meaning was to emerge later.

At this point, I was eager to be finished with the past life. Perhaps Tom sensed this too as he shifted his questions in a different direction.

Chapter Four
Interlude:
With Fortune

"On the count of three, let go of all of this and move up with Fortune. Put your arms around him and ask him what relationship Robbie Winston, Theodore Olson, and Clark Carter have had in any of your lifetimes."

"He says I've known them all before."

Curiously, Tom did not ask further about any past-life connections with these three men in my present life. As for Andrew Petrovski, Tom seemed content to consider the past-life connection with him in England as complete unto itself. Tom continued his questioning but in a different direction.

"Ask him what the mission is for the rest of this present lifetime and if it will be here in the United States or elsewhere in the world?"

I wasn't sure what Tom meant by "mission." I assumed that he meant my purpose in life. To call it a "mission" sounded pretentious but at the same time somewhat intriguing as it implied being sent on it by someone. I wondered whom.

"He's kind of cryptic, says it touches many parts of the world."

"So you're going to do a lot of traveling?"

"It's not clear whether it's traveling in fact, or metaphorically."

"Are you going to become a writer?"

"There'll be a lot of writing involved, but I'm not a 'writer.'" By this I meant a fiction writer.

"Will you write about different countries?"

"About mysteries."

"You're to become a mystery writer, then?"

"Mysteries of life."

Writing the stories of other people's travels in this past life and Fortune's prediction that I would write about mysteries in my present life did not seem to have an obvious corollary at the time, but writing, and particularly writing about what might be called "mysteries," did appear sometime later. So not only was this yet another link between past and present lives, but also Fortune was absolutely correct in his prediction.

Tom moved on to other questions.

"Are you ever going to go back to Africa to live?"

I had mentioned in conversation with Tom about the years I lived in Africa and the importance of the place to me, but he asked this question of Fortune without any pre-session prompting from me.

"For some reason I don't get any answer."

"Tell him that it's important. Ask if there is something pulling you back there."

"The pull is strong, he says. There's a reason for it and it'll become clear later."

"Are you going to be remarried?"

"Yes."

"Will you live here or elsewhere?"

"It won't be in any one place. We will be traveling."

"You'll travel with your husband? Is he going to be

wealthy, and is he going to be—"

"He says I don't really want to know that."

"Will you marry soon?"

"He says sooner than I would have expected."

I was not married at the time that I did this session but Fortune proved correct here again for I did remarry, and sooner than I would have expected.

"Ask him if there's any other special message he has for you at this time."

At this point in the session, the recorder stopped. Afterwards, I looked at this life, as Fortune suggested, and could see other connections with my current life. I had wanted so much to travel back then and hardly did. Going across the channel from England to Amsterdam hadn't constituted for me the kind of adventure I had in mind then. However, in my present lifetime I've been able to travel and live in parts of Asia, Europe, and Africa. Even as a child, I did much traveling with my family.

Did I choose this present family, then, and the circumstances that allowed me the travel opportunities I craved? Perhaps my studying Asian languages and then cultural anthropology in my college years was also motivated by this fascination with other ways of living in the world. On the other hand, one might argue that I fell into these fields first and created a past-life scenario later to explain them. Does it matter? If, as some people think, all history is occurring at the same time on different planes, then such questions about cause and effect would be understood quite differently.

For example, perhaps the fact that I died by drowning

in the English lifetime doesn't explain my current penchant for swimming nor, in reverse, does my interest in swimming make me concoct a past life in which I die by drowning. Perhaps it is rather that on several different but simultaneously occurring planes of existence, I just happen to be managing water with different degrees of success.

There was also the issue of my friendship with Andrew. In the past life, he told me stories of his travels, providing me with an outlet for my own frustrated desire for adventure. In my present incarnation, he was the particular friend who was the catalyst to start me on these past-life journeys.

After this second past-life session, I believed I could very well have been both Rita of eighteenth-century rural Mexico and Susan of nineteenth-century urban England, as well as any number of other people I didn't know of yet. I sought whatever thread it was within me that remained intact throughout the passage of time, despite superficial differences. Was this the soul? And did the soul actually remain intact, or was it undergoing some evolution or growth of its own throughout the various incarnations? Perhaps the soul is complete in itself and these separate lives are fractions of that whole. Reliving past lives, then, could serve as a means of claiming the parts and incorporating them into one's whole being.

I had always wondered about that part of me in which guilt and loneliness exist alongside service to others—what seemed to be Rita's contribution to a complete soul. And after this session as Susan, I was able to accept my lively, vivacious, adventuresome self, along with the argumentative and fearful part of my nature that she also personified. Getting to know myself this way was a satisfying exercise. I felt richer and fuller for incorporating several lives rather than just the present one.

I was, however, reluctant to proceed because of a prejudice against certain kinds of psychotherapy, including past-life work, when it is considered therapy. To me "therapy" means starting with an assumption of deficiency, ailment, or inadequacy which one then attempts to correct. I preferred to think of reliving past lives less as curative treatment and more as an enriching life experience. Rather than seeing myself as a patient, I saw myself as an explorer or adventurer. In the end, my objections to the therapeutic model were outweighed by my curiosity. I arranged to see Tom again.

Chapter Five
As Bethany in Helvetia

The third session began with the usual induction routine, or rather more specifically, Tom's usual induction routine. I had learned from my reading that there are many ways of inducing hypnosis. Most methods seem to include some directions for general physical relaxation and guided visualization with closed or fixated eyes. Hypnotists may differ in style, some being more permissive and others more authoritarian.

Induction has two aspects. One is the subject's entering into a hypnotic trance and the second is the hypnotist's determining that the subject is hypnotized, usually by means of observing eye movements and muscle tone. Tom's style seemed to work very well for me and apparently he was able to ascertain when I was hypnotized. Now as he proceeded to hypnotize me, I relaxed into the familiarity of the words and the tone of his voice.

"You are now up with your master. And I want you to tell me what's going on."

"He's sitting on his stone meditating. Now he's getting up, and we can embrace each other. He asks why I have come."

"All right. Ask him if he is going to be your permanent master."

"He says he will try to answer any questions. If he can't, he'll try to help find somebody who can. He says there are other past lives that will be helpful if looked at."

"Ask him which ones they are so we know where to go."

"He says to find the one that has Fred in it and to go back a long time to a very early life."

Fred is my son in this present life. I don't remember specifically asking about seeking out a past-life connection life with Fred so I was interested that Fortune suggested doing so.

"How will we identify it?"

"It will not be the first lifetime, but one of the earliest that has significance for my current one."

"Okay. That we can understand. Verbalize the other questions you want to ask him and then give me the answers so we can record them."

"I would like to know more about the 'mission' of this lifetime. He says he told me before that I don't need to know more now and that it's not a question he even needs to refer to somebody else. I should be patient and it will become clear."

"Will it become clear shortly?"

"Yes. Little by little, but all the time. He also says I need more faith and patience."

"Ask him if he will help you develop that."

"He says yes, of course, but I need to do a lot of the work myself and I shouldn't look for an easy way."

"You understand and accept that?"

"Mm-hmh."

"What other questions do you want to ask? I believe he said that you would remarry. Is that correct?"

"He says yes."

"Will it be within three years?"

"He says that's one of the questions for faith and patience. I don't need to know the answer now."

"I see. Ask him if you will become an author and lecturer."

"He says very definitely."

"And in what field will you be working?"

"He says it has to do with mysteries and what brings people together from different backgrounds."

"Ask him if you are to work with me in the future, in teaching people to live according to the tenets and practices of the golden age."

I didn't like Tom's talking of a "golden age." The essence of it, as he had explained it in previous conversation, was a world of people living in love. This was a glorious vision to aspire to. But his calling it "the golden age" made it sound to me like a tacky retirement home.

"He says for some time, yes."

"But eventually you will be on your own? Or will you be working with your husband?"

"He says to leave husbands out of the questions for now."

"Okay. Will you be working by yourself?"

"He says it will be my work, that it won't depend on somebody else although I will be working with other people."

I did like very much Fortune's reiterating that my work would be about mysteries and what brings people together from different backgrounds. That was very appealing indeed.

"Will you be spending much time in Africa?"

"Yes, but not exclusively."

"Ask him where Fred will choose to live."

"He's going to do some exploring. In fact, a lot of traveling. And he'll put himself in dangerous places, but that I shouldn't worry. His life is his own."

I was curious to know why Fortune suggested looking at a past-life connection with my son, Fred. That I shouldn't worry about the dangerous places my son might go was strangely both worrisome and then comforting at the same time. Fortune was correct in his prediction that my son would travel. He has already traveled rather extensively, including to some dangerous places but he has been okay. And I have tried my best not to worry.

"Anything else that you'd like to ask him at this time? If it's private, just keep it to yourself."

I was repeating aloud Fortune's answers to Tom's questions as I perceived them. Tom was telepathically attuned enough to pick up a few clues himself without my stating them. However, for the most part, what Fortune told me was for my own hearing alone and I could choose what to say aloud. I noticed that, although I was more eager to please under hypnosis and therefore quite willing to answer most questions, there were some things I did keep to myself, the only disadvantage being that as they were not recorded, I had to depend on my memory to remember them later.

"I feel like I'm spinning, like he's spinning me."

"Ask him why he is doing that to you."

"To shake everything up a bit, he says."

"I see. Ask him if he can help you handle the emotional catharsis you're going through as we do this work."

"He says all he can do is tell me to trust that I won't be given anything more than I can handle."

Although I could clearly visualize Fortune, I could not picture his mouth moving as he answered my questions put to him. It was as if he communicated them to me without actually speaking, and sometimes the answers seemed to come not from him at all but from myself. In whatever manner the answers came to me they did have the ring of truth though, so I didn't waste much time trying to detect their actual source. Even with more time, I suspected much would remain a mystery to me.

"Is there anything else?"

"He thinks he's pretty good as a guide and I shouldn't be dissatisfied. He says that I want easy answers sometimes and I need to work."

"Mm-hmh. He sounds as though he's a very good friend."

"He says he's tough. He may not give me what I want, but for sure he'll give me what I need."

"Ask him if you've known Clark in a previous life."

Clark was a co-worker and close friend of mine. We taught together and had begun a project to start a new school together.

"He says yes, but he doesn't know how to direct me to that life."

"Ask him if you should continue your present association with Clark. Should you attempt your project with him? Will it be worthwhile for you or should you get into something else?"

"He says all I need to do is get it going. The rest of what I'll be doing will start happening then as I finish setting it up."

"Not try to maintain the day-to-day work?"

"He says if I want to I can, but I'll be too busy with the new work."

"Anything else now or should we move to the time where you were in a lifetime with Fred?"

"Go to the lifetime with Fred."

"All right. Thank him for me and for his help and his guidance. Tell him I appreciate getting acquainted with him."

"He says he doesn't mean to be difficult but sometimes it's necessary for me."

"Mm-hmh. I think we can both understand that. On the count of three, without any stress, I want you to say goodbye to Fortune for the time being and move forward to where you are fifteen years of age in the lifetime with Fred. One . . . two . . . three. Where are you now?"

"Outdoors."

"Are you male or female?"

"Female. I don't see Fred."

"No, you wouldn't necessarily at this time. Do you know what country you are living in?"

"No, maybe . . ."

"Just open your mind and let it come in."

"I'm in a field."

I was seeing a steep hillside with small wildflowers. I thought if I knew where the flowers came from, I could tell which country it was. In the distance, there were snow-covered mountains with jagged peaks. I recognized this landscape as similar to one illustrated in the book *Heidi* and the name "Helvetia" came to me as well, but my present mind didn't trust it.

"Do you know what year it is?"

"15 something . . . 73, maybe."

"All right. Do you live with your mother and father?"

"I can't see a mother and father."

"You're speaking very softly today. Can you talk louder for me, please?"

"I'm living with other people."

"I see. What are you doing there?"

"Scrubbing. It's a stone building. I know it but I can't see it right now."

"Mm-hmh. You're out in the meadow right now?"

"Yes."

"Are you just standing there enjoying it or what are you doing?"

"Sitting in the meadow. It's green and warm."

"Is it summertime?"

"Spring, and it's beautiful. I live down the hill."

"Are you a happy child?"

"Yes."

I had a little difficulty with this question because

although I was happy for the moment there on the hillside, the rest of the time I didn't even want to think about the issue of my happiness. I said "yes" because I knew it would cause less trouble. My present mind knew by now that Tom would have pursued the issue had I said I was unhappy. Of course, the whole purpose in exploring a past life was to pursue whatever issues came up, but at the same time I shied away from anything uncomfortable.

"All right. On the count of three, without tension of any kind, I want you to move forward to the house where you stay and describe the people there. One . . . two . . . three. You're now in the house?"

I hesitated to answer because the word "house" was not the appropriate word for the large church building I was seeing. Also, my present mind was busy trying to place the church historically. But the momentum of this past life continued to mount without any regard for my present mind's urge to verify what I was seeing and experiencing.

"It's a large stone building with windows and light. It's not a house."

"Is it a castle?"

"No, some sort of church."

"Are there people around you?"

"Not right now. I'm by myself."

"How are you dressed?"

"In something like a sack."

That's exactly what it was, and made of very coarse, stiff material. After many washings, it had gotten less scratchy, but it was still a primitive way of dressing. There were no sleeves and it was very loose on my body, coming down only as far as the knees, so I was rather exposed.

"Is that all you have on?"

"Yes. I'm scrubbing the stones to make a clean floor."

"I see. Is this a Catholic church, and are you a novice nun?"

The words "novice nun" rang a bell, but it had nothing to do with the likes of me.

"I'm just a girl."

"Let's move forward to where you're with other people. Are they male or female?"

"They're women. They're coming up the hill, back home. I still have water all over on the floor."

"Are you concerned about that?"

"Mm-hmh."

"How are these women dressed?"

"They have long dark clothes. They're very serious, but one of them, Sister Elizabeth, is very nice, always kind to me, and it doesn't matter if I finish the cleaning."

I spoke of this one woman. I was trying to see if I could make her out amongst the others, as they approached. I was relieved to see she was coming.

"I want you to move forward in time now to where you are with this woman, Sister Elizabeth, but first of all, what is your name? Do you know that?"

"I don't know which name. I had another name before. Bethany, that's what they call me."

"What was your original name?"

"I gave it up."

"Are you a novitiate in training to become a nun?"

"I think that's the plan, but I'm not sure it's my plan."

There was talk about my doing this, but for the most part it involved the other girls my age, not me.

"Do you think it would be worthwhile to go back to where you were before you were sent to the church and find out what happened?"

It must have been obvious I was uncomfortable with this suggestion because I didn't answer right away and I was squirming a lot in my seat.

"You don't want to go back? Did something horrible happen to your family? Now, without any stress or strain and no emotion, simply as an observer, don't allow yourself to become emotionally upset now . . ."

"I don't want to talk about it."

My present mind was being called into service with this question or, perhaps I should say, into a dominant position because it seemed that although I was continually operating on two selves or minds simultaneously, at any given moment one or the other minds would predominate. Whenever I was predominantly in the past-life mind, I felt more deeply hypnotized, more in some other space and time, whereas when more in my present mind, I felt barely hypnotized and quite aware of the fact that I was merely lying down following Tom's instructions. Whenever the instructions pertained to the hypnosis procedure itself such as to move forward in time, or whenever mention was made of my current life, I always felt pulled back to present-mind awareness.

Otherwise, I easily sank into the past life. Nevertheless, I was never in past or present to the exclusion of the other. They seemed to flow into each other such that it would be difficult at times to pinpoint just which mind was primary. It was usually upon shifting back to the present that I was made aware by the contrast that I had been more deeply involved in the past-life.

I reeled at Tom's suggestion to go back to my earlier childhood. I did not know what had happened to make me not want to relive it. Instead, I must have been reacting to a lost memory, a reaction that would seem to support the idea that emotions can remain intact long after their original causes have been forgotten or lost to another lifetime. Just as a person might keep from consciousness a potentially unpleasant memory from an earlier part of the life, one might also try to keep from one's conscious mind certain painful memories from previous lifetimes. This psychological mechanism known as repression seemed to be operating here across the boundaries of birth and death. I resisted the suggestion to review what I somehow knew might be painful. But as one function of the past-life work is to bring such repressions to resolution, Tom persisted, firmly but sensitively.

"Without any emotion, simply as though you were observing a film, move to where you're five years of age."

"Another woman was taking care of me, but she can't do it any longer."

"I see."

"She was the one that found me."

"Had something happened to your parents before

this?"

"I don't know. The woman says she found me when I was a baby. I was just left in the street."

"As an infant?"

"Yes."

"And now she's sending you to the Catholic nunnery?"

"She says they'll take care of me there."

"Okay. What name did she give you?"

"She just calls me 'little one.'"

"So when you get to the nunnery, then they give you the name Bethany?"

"They'll give me a name."

Never before had I had such a concrete personal experience confirming the well-known cultural observation that naming confers a place in society. It wasn't clear whether something had also happened to my parents but it was clear that I had suffered and was abandoned as unwanted, unclaimed, and nameless in the world.

"All right. Then let us move again to where you are fifteen years of age. Are you a very attractive young lady?"

After a long pause, I said, "I don't know."

"Don't you ever look in the mirror?"

"No, there aren't any mirrors."

"Are you a fairly big girl? Are you heavy or thin?"

"Small."

"Mm-hmh. Anything else you'd like to tell me or shall we move to where you are eighteen years of age? One . . . two . . . three. Where are you now?"

"I'm with the woman."

"Is she Sister Elizabeth?"

She was Sister Elizabeth but my present mind was untrusting of this name because of its being my name in my current life. I thought I might be making it up, so my voice here was asking a question rather than making a statement. I think that the name chosen for me—Bethany—was taken from her name, Elizabeth, because she "took me under her wing."

"She mothered you during the time you were in the convent?"

"Yes, she's been very good. She says I don't have to stay if I don't want to, but I don't really have anywhere else to go."

"You're not particularly anxious to become a nun."

"I'd like to stay with her but I also have a want to see a bit more of the world."

"By the way, what city do you live near? Do you know?"

"Mirages or Morge . . . or something like that."

"All right. Is Sister Elizabeth the superior sister at the convent?"

I wasn't sure of the title of her position, as I hadn't paid much attention to the hierarchies there. She was in charge, however, so I guess that made her superior. It was an issue with some people but I didn't have to pay any attention to discussions about it or about anything else for that matter, except for what Sister Elizabeth offered to me for my consideration.

"Do you feel that this is a lifetime where you will

meet Fred? Have you met him yet? Remember that he may appear as female in this lifetime."

"I don't know."

There was some charge around this question. The name "Fred" seemed out of place in this lifetime but something else, which I cannot describe, an essence, perhaps, seemed to be very much present.

"Okay. Let's move forward to where you are nineteen years of age. One . . . two . . . three. Where are you now?"

"On the way down the mountainside."

"Mm-hmh."

"It's a slim path and Sister Elizabeth is coming with me part of the way. She wants to go as far as she can. She says she will visit me, that I should send word when I settle somewhere."

"And you're going into a city?"

"I haven't been there before. She's told me that if I stay on the path and go all the way down and just keep asking for the city, I'll find it. I'm glad to be going but I'm kind of scared."

"That's pretty understandable. Let's move forward to where you're in the city, unless something of importance has happened."

There was a very long pause here. I had a very difficult time moving ahead so quickly because it was hard to let go of Sister Elizabeth. She knew that she ought to allow me to go into the city and find out for myself what it was all about, but she also was very protective of me and reluctant to send me off. She went further down the mountain with me than she had intended but finally she did say goodbye, wished me well, then blessed me. She was a heavy woman and the climb back up was going to be hard for her.

As she turned to go, I felt that we had merged somehow. It was indeed very difficult to collect myself. I stood there for some time watching her go, but she never once turned around to look back after she started up the hill. It was my remembering the benediction that she sent along with me as we parted that allowed me finally to continue on my way.

"I'm in the city. It's dirty."

"Are there people? Are you near them or with them?"

"Sitting on the ground beside a stone wall and . . . I don't like to say . . ."

"It's important that you do say it. Go ahead."

"I have a cup. I'm begging."

"Mm-hmh. You have no money so this is the only way you can get enough to eat and live on, as you get started. That's understandable. Are people giving you money?"

"Yes, but it's hard."

"That's all right. You're allowing false pride to come in. Release your emotions so that this will be gone from your life, but don't do it in such a way that it affects you right now."

I'm sure my present mind could have made sense of this last suggestion had I tried, but I barely even noticed it as I was too involved in the past life.

"I don't like to ask people."

"I know you don't, but you have to do it. Later on

you'll be able to give money in return to somebody else that needs help."

"I wait 'til it's dark and then I cry."

"Where do you sleep?"

"I stay where I am."

"You sleep there on the street?"

"Yes."

"Where do you eat?"

"There's an inn. When I have money, I go there and have some stew and bread, but they don't like to see me."

"All right. Let's move forward a few months to see what happens."

"I'm coming back up the hill. I want to go back to the sisters."

"Have you been living on the street all this time?"

"I would have left sooner. I didn't want Elizabeth to see . . ."

I was going to say "how ragged and dirty I had become."

"Have the men had anything to do with you?"

Here I was crying.

"Hang on just a minute." Tom handed me a Kleenex.

"They beat me."

"Have they sexually assaulted you or have you sold yourself to them?"

"No, I fight, but I don't like fighting."

"Did anybody befriend you at all?"

"No."

"Is there anything wrong with your appearance?"

"I'm raggedy."

"Have you ever looked in a mirror and seen your face?"

"No."

"Is there a reason for that?"

"I don't want to see."

"Is there something wrong with your face?"

"I don't know. I think there must be."

"Did anyone ever say anything about it?"

"People look at me and then they turn away. Maybe it's why my mother threw me out."

I don't think I had a clue as to what I looked like, nor do I think I was bright enough to have figured out yet what the problem was merely by observing the reactions of others. I hadn't seen mirrors so I couldn't see my face. I could only see the rest of me, which I knew looked pretty shabby, but other than that okay. Tom's questions made me think and put two and two together. Perhaps my mother threw me out because I was disfigured.

"Did you, by any chance, meet the person yet who is Fred in this present lifetime?"

"I want to think it's Elizabeth, but . . . no, I haven't met him."

"Let's move forward now to where you're back up at the convent. You're now with Sister Elizabeth?"

"Yes."

"Has she taken you back in?"

"Of course."

"Ask her . . ."

I sighed.

"Just relax now, just relax. You're now back home."

I was so full of emotion. The tears were streaming down my face. It was home, that was true, and it was also obviously the only place that I could be so there was a very intense melancholy that colored this nice homey feeling—that it was both home and confinement.

"Ask her if there is something wrong with your appearance that causes people not to accept you."

"She says yes, but that it wasn't my fault. She also says that people don't see the soul."

"Okay. Ask her if she is Fred in this present incarnation."

"She says yes!"

My present mind tried to make sense of this. How could anyone in the 1500s know that she would reincarnate hundreds of years later to a specific person? This one comment made my mind spin around strange notions of time. Tom continued.

"Mm-hmh! Are you now going to become a nun or will you just live and work there?"

"She says I can do as I like, and if I want to leave again, that's all right too."

"She is a beautiful lady, isn't she?"

"Yes."

"All right. Let's move forward. You're almost twenty years of age now, aren't you?"

"I'm older."

"How old are you?"

"She says she doesn't know how old I am because she doesn't know when I was born."

"All right. Then let's move forward to where you're

twenty-five."

Again my present mind tried to puzzle this out. Who or what was directing me to see this life? It could not have been me because I didn't know how old I was to be able to go to a specific age. Where did all this come from? Nevertheless, I somehow was catapulted to myself at age twenty-five in that life.

"I'm still there and have become a sister."

"Mm-hmh."

"She's been letting me do a lot of the work in the church. She says this is the best place for me to be. But that I can still leave anytime, that I may want to have my own church somewhere else."

"How old is Sister Elizabeth?"

"I don't know. She seems ancient, probably in her fifties."

This comment on her being ancient was not a young person's view of someone older but rather an attempt to describe the ageless quality she had. Maybe she was an old soul, as they say.

"Are you healthy also, or do you have a lot of illnesses?"

"I'm healthy."

"Is there anything else?"

"She says that whether she's with me or not that she will always love me. She will always watch out for me."

"How do you get along with the other nuns? Do they accept you all right?"

"Yes. There's room for me here."

"Have you ever looked in a mirror or glanced at your

reflection in a pool of water?"

"She showed me a mirror once."

"What do you look like?"

This is a curious thing. As I recall, Sister Elizabeth never dealt with what I looked like before I went away to the city. In fact, she rather purposefully removed from my seeing any mirrors or reflecting surfaces when I was growing up. But when I came back, she drew me aside one day to introduce me to the reality of my appearance. I wonder if she had hoped that would happen when I went away and she wouldn't have had to do it herself. Although she had tried very hard to protect me, she now decided I had better know because if I knew I could try to overcome the issue and understand why people reacted as they did. Now I wonder if it was only Tom's questions that prompted her to do so. But then we get into the whole issue of time, again. Had she done so at the time on account of some little unaccountable time-warped voice that asked her about it, a voice that came from centuries in the future? Intriguing thought, but I digress.

"My face is crooked. I have a large birthmark. It's purple and orange."

"Mm-hmh."

"I don't like to talk about it, but she helps me with that too."

"She certainly gives you a lot of love. Does she ever hold you?"

"Oh yes."

She was the only person who ever touched me other than those that beat and poked at me.

"Where do you sleep there? Do you have your own bed?"

"A straw bed in one of the rooms. The straw sticks out and sometimes wakes me up but every morning when Elizabeth asks if I've slept well, I have to say yes."

What I meant was that I didn't feel like complaining about it because Elizabeth's kindly concern was so consuming that it just swallowed up the problem.

"Do you have any special friends among the other nuns?"

"No."

"Anything else you'd like to tell me?"

"I don't think so."

"All right. Let's move forward now to where you're forty years of age on the count of three, without any strain. One . . . two . . . three. Where are you now? Still in the convent?"

"Yes."

"Is Elizabeth still alive?"

"Yes, but she's very sick. She's wasting away, getting thinner and thinner. She's still as kind, but her mind isn't all there."

"Do you take care of her?"

"Of course."

"Are you reasonably happy?"

There was a long pause before I answered.

"I don't like that question."

"Will you ask Sister Elizabeth what year it is now?"

"I don't want to ask her anything."

"Why?"

"She's so weak. I don't want to trouble her."

"Okay. Shall we move forward then to where you're forty-five? What has happened?"

"She's dead."

"Sister Elizabeth has died? But she led a good life, didn't she? And she was a very loving, kind and wonderful person. Will you continue to live there? There'll be a new mother superior but she'll keep you on, won't she?"

I was absorbed in my plan and didn't notice this last question.

"I know what I'm going to do. I told Sister Elizabeth but she said not to do it."

"What's that?"

"I told her when she dies, I'm going to die too. I'm going to climb up the church and jump."

"Are you going to do it very soon?"

"Yes."

"All right then. On the count of three, you're going to move forward to the last day of your life in this incarnation. Remember you will not have crossed over into spirit yet. As an absolute command, you will feel no pain or emotion. You will experience this entire situation objectively, without trauma of any kind. One . . . two . . . three. Where are you now?"

I don't remember consciously hearing these instructions to remain calm but they were undoubtedly necessary, as I was breathing hard and sighing audibly throughout them.

"I'm waiting for the sun to go down so no one can see me."

I was distressed and crying as I spoke.

"I know she said not to do it, but I can't stay alive."

As my past self was undergoing the wrenching stress of this inner conflict, the absolute certainty of my decision to kill myself and the equally powerful burden of my promise not to, I felt a severe pain in my present body. It was as if my heart were being squeezed shut.

"You need to get rid of this long-repressed anguish."

"She'll have to forgive me!"

"She will forgive you."

When I cried out, I was already climbing up the side of the church building. It was crudely built and stones stuck out in enough places that I could easily get a foothold with each step. I could feel the cold night air on my skin, which was hot with emotion and tears. This contrast kept me alert and focused as I made my way to the roof.

"Now, without any strain, simply as though you were an observer, I want you to leave your physical body and find yourself in spirit, just a few moments after experiencing death.

One . . . two . . . three. Where are you now in relationship to your body? Are you looking down on it?"

"Yes."

"Is Sister Elizabeth there with you, in spirit?"

"No."

"Are you happier now?"

I certainly was feeling relieved although there was still a small part of my mind monitoring the anguish of the last day. I had worried whether physically I would be able to bear such devastating emotion, so my relief was due both to a gradual subsiding of the pain in my chest and the realization that something of me was going to survive after all.

"What have you learned from this lifetime that can be applicable in your present life? Shall we take a quick trip up to see Fortune again?"

"I want to look just a little while longer at my body down there."

"All right."

I felt a need to absorb the fact of this death, and to feel the difference between the soul and the physical self. I certainly felt freer, less encumbered having left the physical behind. I could see the body as merely a lifeless shell, while the "real" me adjusted to being in spirit. I didn't, however, want to witness anybody's reaction to seeing the crumpled heap on the ground, so, as the dark night faded and it began to get light, I was ready to leave the scene.

"Are you ready now? On the count of three, I want you to move up. How's Fortune doing now?"

"He's coming to me and holding his arms out."

This was, to put it mildly, a most welcome change from his previous, rather restrained demeanor. I was very moved by this gesture.

"He says I've done well, been brave."

"Ask him if he will help you understand what you were to learn in reliving that lifetime so that you can utilize it effectively in your present incarnation."

"He says knowing about it . . . will be very freeing."

"Mm-hmh! You know now that Fred was a beautiful person in a previous lifetime. Ask him if Fred will be as good for you in this one as when his spirit was Sister Elizabeth."

"He says Fred now has his own life, that I should let him go to live it. He says that I know it and that Fred knows it as well, at some level, but that I should not burden him with all of this."

"And give him some of the same love and affection that Sister Elizabeth gave you."

"He says I've been doing that."

"I'm sure you have."

"He says now I know why I've been doing it."

Tom proceeded to bring me out of hypnosis. I had been so engrossed in the past life this time that the transition to the present was both slow and labored. I was on the verge of tears from emotional exhaustion.

My present mind, which usually accompanied these journeys into the past lives as a monitor, seemed barely there during this session, especially at the climax, when climbing the church wall to commit suicide. Obviously, I was able to hear and answer the questions that Tom put to me, but the connection at that point between the past life and the present was tenuous. The link that usually existed between my experience of the past and my awareness of the present had narrowed, at that critical point, to a very thin and fragile thread that threatened to snap at any minute. In spite of the instruction to observe it all without emotion, I felt tremendous anguish at that moment.

Later, I was able to see that such extreme emotional devastation requires a very well-trained, sensitive hypnotist to get one through it. Sensitivity is necessary to be able to ascertain the severity of emotional trauma and sufficient training is essential to know how to manage the crisis.

This incident brought up another question about the process of the work. I wondered just how much emotion was advisable while experiencing a past life. Although a certain amount of reliving the emotion was apparently necessary to dissipate unresolved charge affecting the present, it occurred to me that, perhaps, one could suffer doubly repressed emotions if a particular situation was experienced for a second time without full understanding. Could one, then, be worse off than before?

I asked Tom about this since, after all, he always said to "observe without any stress or strain" and yet seemed to think a certain amount of emotion was necessary to free oneself from negative karma. Tom's answer was that it was necessary to feel the strong emotions that arose naturally so as to understand how important any particular situation had been, but that the process of reliving complete lives in this manner also allowed one to place any particular emotionally-charged situation into the context of a whole life thereby gaining a broader perspective. The bird's-eye view gained by looking back from another lifetime allowed a degree of detachment as one relived and resolved because the reliving was accomplished primarily through the power of the mind rather than the physical body. One was then allowed to go, unencumbered and free, through one's present life without hidden agendas from the past.

I was also concerned about the relative accessibility of this kind of insight gained by reliving a past life. It seemed to me that this knowledge was such powerful stuff that there must be some principle of nature that prevented just anybody at anytime from tapping into it without preparation. If knowing one's past lives could stir up the kind of crazy-making confusion I was going through, it seemed to me that some self-protective principle of nature must function to keep people from stumbling upon such jarring insights.

Yet it seemed anyone could do a past-life session without special expertise. And, after all, everyone is entitled to learn whatever he or she can, however difficult or easy. There certainly need not be any exclusive group of people who alone are privacy to this experience. I wondered why more people weren't taking advantage of this learning process.

After all, it wasn't physically difficult for me to drive to where Tom worked, be quiet, and be hypnotized. And again, some people have past-life memories involuntarily without going to the trouble of finding outside assistance such as hypnosis, meditation, drugs, or acupuncture. I had heard of people for whom visiting a place or meeting a certain person triggered memories of other lives. So it wasn't clear to me whether this was all meant to be occult knowledge or not.

Were there not also only certain permissible contexts

in which to do this? Could one "play" casually with past-life regression or only work at it in formal sessions? And what would a formal work session require? It seemed we were dealing with a special process that released powerful revelations, all of which commanded a level of respect and care.

When I asked Tom about this, he said that his guiding principle had been simply to help people. He seemed to trust in whatever brought people to work with him. Meanwhile, he continually sought to improve his own manner of participation in the process, refining his techniques as he went along. That seemed right, but too simple. On my own, I kept struggling with these issues, assuming it was much more complicated than that.

I had a lot to think about from this past-life connection with my son. For one thing, I wanted so much to talk with him about it but he was not at all interested, in fact adamantly refused to hear of it, at least for the time being. I realize I had to respect Fortune's advice about allowing him to live his own life and not burdening him with what I had discovered. For myself, if indeed Sister Elizabeth was an earlier version of Fred, I could understand the foundation for the strong bond we had between us. I had always assumed that was a natural mother-child bond but I came to learn that such a bond is not always present.

After several sessions and my ongoing attempts to find meaning and order both in the content and the process, I felt less willing to talk about it to others than I had before. It became an increasingly private quest. After the first session, I had felt tossed about by the waves it produced in me. Now I felt as if I were slowly finding my sea legs. I could carry on with a little less fear and a little more confidence even though the going was still rather rough and choppy.

Chapter Six
Interlude:
Conversation with Fortune

I met Tom again but I was nervous about reliving any more past lives after the trauma of the last one. What would happen this time? Were there any guarantees that I wouldn't break under the strain of possibly even greater emotional distress? Tom assured me that any extremely emotional circumstance encountered in a past life somehow causes the person to wake up from the session. But, in all his years of work, even this built-in safety mechanism had never been called into play.

Tom suggested it might be a good time to do a bonding session—a re-creation, under hypnosis, of the birth experience—either one's own birth or the birth of one's child. I knew of rebirthing as a reliving of one's own actual birth, however unpleasant it may have been. By contrast, Tom's bonding session was designed to manufacture a whole new birth experience. This re-created birth would be natural, easy, and relatively painless, allowing a positive connection to be made between mother and child no matter what the original experience had been. I knew that bonding at birth was important from my work in childbirth teaching, but I was disturbed by the idea of inventing a bond where it hadn't occurred. That seemed like tampering with nature. Wasn't it better to learn to accept what cannot be changed? Or was it perhaps possible and okay to change it? Or maybe this would just be a new interpretation to add to the first?

Tom also did hypnosis sessions for pregnant women before they gave birth, full of positive suggestions for easier deliveries. That made sense to me; it was this after-the-fact bonding that baffled me. Anyway, I thought it unnecessary in my case, as my birthing experiences as both a child and a mother had been positive. I didn't think they could have been improved upon in any way.

Nevertheless, Tom said that it didn't take long to do a session and that it would be easy and relaxing. I agreed it might just calm my nerves, which were still frazzled from the emotional strain of the last past-life session. Tom hypnotized me and then directed me through an easy birthing of my child. There seemed to be no discrepancy between the experience of the real birth and Tom's re-created one. The bonding session did not demand much emotional energy nor did it take a lot of time so in the end it served as a relaxing interlude.

My interest in the past-life work began now to widen to include aspects other than what I experienced. I was curious to know, for example, about the role of the hypnotist. I asked Tom about his part in the process—what a session was like for him, what difficulties there were, how he knew what to ask and when, and so forth. He said that with every session he becomes deeply involved, often finding himself able to see and hear what the person is seeing and hearing. At the same time, he must maintain the technical details, such as keeping an overview of the session and the timing of any part of it, monitoring the recording and especially modulating his voice, which he considers his strongest tool.

Sometimes subjects have been hard to hypnotize. Sometimes these have been people who are fearful, under extreme stress or tension, or too busy analyzing and evaluating to relax into hypnosis. But it isn't always clear why, even when a person seems keenly interested, either the hypnotic state or past lives remain elusive. This seemed to be the case with my friend Andrew Petrovski. I had passed along to him not only the contact information for Tom Thomason but also had told him what came of my first sessions. Andrew made an appointment for himself. However, it seemed he was not a good hypnotic subject. For some reason, he just couldn't be hypnotized. I don't know how many times he tried. It is possible there wasn't a compatibility between himself as subject and Tom Thomason as hypnotist.

Trust between hypnotist and subject is essential. As for knowing what to ask and when, Tom said he found it best to rely on the direction of the guides, both his own and those of his subjects.

I asked Tom how someone else might find a hypnotist to conduct past-life sessions. Tom suggested consulting some of the professional bodies, such as the Association for Past Life Research and Therapy or the various associations of hypnotists, not for a recommendation but merely for a referral. The final decision to work together would still rest with the hypnotist and client as a matter of personal choice and mutual trust.

I considered preparing to become a past-life

hypnotist myself. I even conjured up a plan of becoming an apprentice to Tom. Tom was not encouraging, but he did loan me some reading material on hypnosis.

I found more books on past lives and reincarnation and began reading voraciously again. I was also interested in verifying any specific information that came through my own sessions. I looked at maps of Switzerland, for example, searching for the town of Mirages or Morge or any town with a similar name. Trying to locate the town and the convent in the steep hills above the town was not easy. Without an exact spelling of the name and without an exact year for a historical search, I have not been able, so far, to find the convent. There is the substantial town of Morges in the Morges district of Switzerland on Lake Geneva. However, the topography of that area does not resemble the topography in the past life. So the search continues.

In my reading, I came across a way that might prove I wasn't making this all up myself. Suppose someone in my present life were to be found also in a past life. Then suppose that person, on his or her own, did a past-life session with Tom specifically seeking one where they had known me. The two past-life stories could then be cross-checked for accuracy. I had read this had been done before both accidentally and on purpose. Tom agreed to try this experiment if a willing subject were found.

I decided to seek out a past-life connection with my friend Clark. We had been friends for years, had worked together and were working towards starting a new school together. We had not gotten very far with it at this point but I felt obliged to continue with the project somehow in spite of obstacles. I had told Clark about the past-life sessions I had already done. He seemed interested enough that I thought he might be willing to try this cross-checking experiment. It turned out that he was not quite that interested so the cross-checking experiment did not happen and I continued to carry on with the explorations on my own.

I made another appointment with Tom. He asked me how I was doing. He never asked this question lightly and during these difficult days my answer was hardly ever light either.

This time I had been having some minor physical complaints such as headaches. Perhaps they were connected with the past-life work and the issues it had raised for me. I had been taking as good care of myself as I could, firmly believing that the body needs to be strong on the physical level to handle work on the metaphysical level. I added to my regimen a regular weight-lifting program, which I had never done before. Both physically and metaphysically, I was dealing with heavy things.

Tom suggested that we ask Fortune for advice on the health problems. He hypnotized me and directed me to Fortune.

"All right. Now I want you to go up with Fortune on the count of three. One . . . two . . . three. How is your friend doing?"

"He's laughing."

"Is he laughing at you or with you?"

"He's kind of chuckling. He's glad to see me. He's

laughing at my persistence. He's saying it's good that I want to keep working at this. It's a kind of stubbornness that's going in a good direction so he's chuckling."

I wasn't at all sure that I agreed with Fortune on this point. If anyone had seriously questioned me about all these sessions, I would have had a hard time justifying the time and energy I was putting into it. I grew up in this time and culture in which skepticism is fashionable and faith, or at least blind faith, is often regarded as an embarrassment. In addition, the materialistic and commercial mind-set of modem life generally limits our faith to what we can touch, taste, smell, see, and hear—and especially buy and sell. All else is suspect. So it is not surprising that I wanted, above all, to find proof.

Fortune's support of my action was welcome but not crucial. I hadn't yet reconciled myself as to who or what Fortune was to be able to take anything he said seriously.

Tom suggested I ask Fortune about the headaches and if I would be able to control them.

"He says *yes.*"

"Tell him we would like to visit some other lives that would be of value to revisit so that it may help you in your present life. Ask him if he has any particular lifetime that he thinks you should go back to. You have discussed one as a male, one going back to a very early lifetime, possibly in Atlantis or Lemuria. Ask him what he thinks."

"He says going back to a very early lifetime is a good idea but it will be difficult to talk about it so maybe now I should take a look at a more recent lifetime just for the practice, and then I could look at the early lifetime later on."

"Ask him what lifetime he thinks you should go to right now."

"He says seeing a lifetime as a male is not so important but if I am curious, that's all right. I could also look at a lifetime when Clark was in my life, which just might be the same lifetime. He says to go to the Clark life and then the rest will come."

Clark Carter and I worked together as teachers and were both very devoted to the work. We thought about starting a new school together and had investigated location, costs, licensing, and so forth. Outside of work we did get together to play music, he on piano and me on flute. Also, his circle of friends and mine overlapped enough that we ran into each other at parties and other events. But it was our joint school project that had propelled me to ask about a past-life connection with him. Unfortunately the timing was not good for starting a new school as several incidents of abuses in private schools were hitting the news just when we were talking to bank people about loans for our project. As a result, we were stymied and ultimately did not pursue the project, partly, I believe, because of what I was about to learn from our past-life connection.

Chapter Seven
As a Sandal-Maker in Ancient Greece

"All right. On the count of three I want you to go back to a lifetime where you knew Clark. One . . . two . . . three. Where are you now? Are you indoors or are you out-of-doors?"

"Outdoors. On some steps."

"Is it a house or large building or an office?"

"Large building."

I saw myself on some broad steps leading up to a very large and important stone building. It looked like a Greek temple from the top of which one could see a long ways off. I was wearing a short, sleeveless "dress" which had pleats below the waist and was loosely bloused above the waist. I was wearing sandals with thongs that came up my calves. I was particularly pleased with my sandals for some reason.

"How old are you?"

"Fifteen."

"Are you male or female?"

"Male."

"What is your name?"

"Anthony."

"What country are you living in?"

"Greece."

"And do you know what year it is?"

"No."

"What are you doing on the steps? Are you alone?"

"I'm waiting."

"What are you waiting for?"

"I'm waiting for my friend to come."

"Is that friend going to be Clark in this lifetime?'

"Maybe."

When I consider this answer of "maybe," it seems to raise again the question of how all this viewing of past lives (if indeed there were past lives) was able to happen. On the one hand, if I were able to drop back in time to watch, like watching a movie of a life, how would I, in that life, know of any future ones and make connections between people? On the other hand, maybe I or some other entity was able to see a bigger picture of all the lives and make such connections. It was a mystery I was not about to solve at that moment.

"All right. Let's move forward to where your friend is there with you. One . . . two . . . three. Is he now there with you?"

"No."

"Where are you now? Are you still on the steps?"

"Yes. I'm sitting down waiting. It's getting dark."

"He hasn't shown up then?"

"No."

"You've waited a long time."

"Yes."

"Are you concerned?"

"Yes."

"Are things peaceful in Greece at this time?"

I didn't quite know how to answer this question.

Things were relatively peaceful where I was, but everyone was agitated. There was talk of war and marches and soldiers. There was a general uneasiness as to whom you could count on as a friend. Any question put by a stranger or even an acquaintance had to be answered carefully.

"I'm not sure. It's okay for me."

"Is your family living there? What city do you live in?"

"Sparta."

"Does your family live there?"

"Yes."

"And you live with them?"

"They live in Sparta. I am in Athens."

"What are you doing there? Are you going to school or are you working or what?"

"I think I want to be a soldier."

The friend I was waiting for, whom I greatly admired, had tried to convince me of the idea. He was older and wiser, or so I thought. He was also good-looking and strong with an air of confidence and charm. I envied him and was captivated by his plan for us to lead exciting lives as soldiers of fortune. But I did have some doubts.

"It is now getting dark. Are you going to wait any longer for your friend or are you going to go back to where you live?"

"I'm not sure where to go."

"Did you just get into Athens?"

"Yes."

"Did your friend come with you from Sparta?"

"No, I was to meet him here, but he hasn't come."

"Do you have any money?"

"A few coins."

I didn't want to reveal exactly how many coins I had in my little bag but the few I had I intended to use only if necessary.

"Let's move forward the next few hours on the count of three. One . . . two . . . three. Where are you now?"

"I've gone around the corner and I'm sleeping. I can't sleep very well but I don't know what else to do. It's dark."

"Let's move forward to the next day and see if you got through the night safely. One . . . two . . . three. What are you doing now?"

"I'm waking up and it's a beautiful day. I don't know what happened to my friend but I can just look around and see what there is to see. I feel better now that it's light."

That was putting it mildly. I had been very scared. I had never been away from home before. I had been counting on my friend to shepherd me in the strange city. I thought it best to wait at the appointed place until he showed up. The building, by its huge size and seeming importance, offered a kind of protection, especially at night. Daylight brought relief from fear and a boost to my self-esteem in that I had managed to make it through the night. I had a bit of a swagger now as I began to walk about with this city at my feet and the freedom to explore it at my whim.

"Let's move forward to where you finally get with

your friend on the count of three. One . . . two . . . three. You're now with your friend. Where are you?"

"I'm not."

"You're not? You're unable to find him?"

"I'm not really looking for him. I don't know where to look. I'm just walking around to see what there is to see. I'm trying not to worry but I don't know quite what to do. It took so long coming here."

"How many days did it take you to come from Sparta to Athens?"

"It was overnight. I got some rides coming."

"What did you ride in?"

"Carts."

They were carts pulled by animals and were a welcome relief from walking. But it wasn't possible to get much sleep bumping along in the back of the carts.

"Are there people around you right now?"

"Yes."

"Ask some people what year it is. Ask somebody that looks intelligent and well-dressed."

Tom paused here and waited before asking, "What do they say?"

"He won't answer. I have to ask somebody else."

I had asked an older man who was traveling with a retinue. He was too well-dressed for me to approach him and so, as I anticipated, he turned up his nose at my impertinence and didn't answer.

"What are you finding out?"

"I'm not finding out very much. People don't know me. They don't want to talk to me."

"Are you dressed differently?"

"Well, a little bit but not that much. It's just that they don't know me."

"Then let's move forward now a week and see what you do. One . . . two . . . three. Where are you now?"

"I'm back at the temple. There's an old man here who says I don't really want to become a soldier. He says maybe it's good my friend didn't come. He was going to help me become a soldier."

Across the top of the steps to the temple was a row of tall columns. The old man sat inside the row of columns and just outside the front door as if to greet everyone that came to the temple. He had noticed me hanging about the temple and wondered what I was doing. When I told him, he grasped the whole situation immediately—that I had come a long way under the spell of my friend who had persuaded me to try the adventurous life of a soldier. He had guessed correctly that I didn't really want to be a soldier, but I was secretly hoping that in the process I might turn out like my friend whom I looked up to literally as well as figuratively.

The old man who had white hair and a long, white beard was the picture of wisdom. He seemed genuinely concerned for me and offered to look out for me, teach me other things besides soldiering. He made it quite clear that he didn't think much of soldiers.

"Ask the old man what year it is. What does he say?"

"He says if I stay with him, he will teach me. He will tell me about the years and how they work. He doesn't want to tell me now."

Any question concerning the year was obviously a ticklish one. People apparently counted the years differently depending on their political or religious allegiances. Somehow what calendar one used indicated one's loyalty in one way or another so this was not something that was lightly discussed.

"You like this old man?"

"Yes, he reminds me of my grandfather."

"You feel that you're going to stay with him?"

I liked the old man and it was clear that he was concerned about me but I also suspected that the more I talked with him the more I might be getting myself into some other kind of adventure with equally dangerous albeit different risks. The old man was apparently connected with the temple and its religious order, which apparently included an educational component. It was the educational part that the old man was trying to interest me in. I didn't know whether I should trust the old man or not.

"I don't know whether I should stay. I think maybe I should go back."

"Let see what happens. One . . . two . . . three. Where are you now?"

"I'm going back."

"To Sparta?"

"To my family, yes."

"Let's move forward to where you're back with your family. One . . . two . . . three. Is everything okay there?"

"Well, yes. My mother is glad to see me. My father says I shouldn't have gone anyway, that my friend isn't reliable."

"What is your name?" Tom asked again.

"Anthony."

"What are your mother's and father's names?"

"Mark."

"What's your mother's name?"

"Herate . . . Heracle . . . Herate, I think."

"Do you have a family name?"

"Family name?"

"Yeah. Do you have a surname, a second part of your name? Your name is Anthony. Is that all you go by?"

"Yes, I'm Mark's son."

"All right. What are you going to do now? What were you doing before you left? Did you work with your father?"

"Yes."

"What does he do?"

"He makes sandals."

"Do you dislike doing that or do you like it?"

"Well, it's okay. I just wanted to go off and be a soldier . . . maybe."

"And have a little adventure?"

"Mm-hmh."

"Are you happy now to be back?"

"Well, I wanted to go. It's okay being back, sure."

"Do you have brothers and sisters?"

"I have a sister. She's younger than I am."

"Ask your father what year it is."

"He says that I should have remembered that we count the years from when Caesar was king."

"Then you're on the old Roman calendar. What year is that?"

"He says he won't tell me because I should have known it but I think it's somewhere around 40 . . . 50 . . . 65?"

"The year 65? This is a long time ago then. Anything else you'd like to tell me? Do you normally get along well with your parents and your sister?"

"Yeah. My mother and my sister are fine. My father gives me a hard time."

"Let's move forward to where you're eighteen and see what happens. One . . . two . . . three. Where are you now?"

"I'm at home with my mother and sister and my father and I'm working with my father. I'm making sandals."

To my present mind, this past life was rather dull so far. I wasn't really interested in reliving the rest of it but it kept moving along anyway.

"What do you do when you're not making sandals? Do you have friends around or girlfriends?"

"There's a girl that comes to the house. She's a friend of my sister."

"Mm-hmh."

"Shyra."

"Is she a beautiful girl?"

"Yes."

"Are you a handsome young man?"

"I don't think she thinks so."

I don't think anybody thought so. My mother loved

me and was very affectionate but my father was not. It seemed I was always disappointing him even though I didn't do anything bad or disrespectful. Probably I just wasn't manly enough. He didn't particularly like my soldiering friend but he may have harbored the same hopes I did about my becoming a soldier—that it would make a man out of me. Meanwhile, his constant reproaches didn't help my already weak self-esteem. I rarely sought out either male friends or possible girlfriends. I came to know Shyra largely because she came to visit my sister.

"Are you big or small for the people around you at eighteen years of age? Are you as big as your father, or bigger?"

"Oh, no. He's bigger than I am. He's taller and . . ." I sighed. "I've grown some but I wish I were taller."

"Are you enjoying making sandals more now?"

"It's not something you enjoy. You just do it."

"Are you interested in Shyra then?"

"Yes."

"But she doesn't give you much time, does she?"

"She's playful with me but only if there's nothing else happening."

She would tease me and seemed to enjoy the fact that I liked her but she didn't take me seriously for a long time.

"Is there anything else you'd like to tell me or shall we move forward to where you're twenty?"

"Sure."

"On the count of three. One . . . two . . . three. Where

are you now?"

"Still making sandals."

"Still making sandals? Are you married now?"

"No."

"Have you ever made any progress with Shyra?"

"She's a good friend."

By this time, she took more interest in me but mainly out of familiarity over the years. She had accepted me as one of the people that made up her life and she didn't tease me except in an affectionate manner. We had become good friends.

"Your friend Clark that you know in this lifetime, is he in that lifetime?"

"I haven't seen him."

"Is that by any chance Shyra?"

"No."

"All right. Maybe he comes into your life a little later. Was it the old man by any chance?"

"No, I think it was my friend that . . . I don't know what happened to him."

"It was the friend that you've never seen or heard from since. Did he live there in Athens or did he live in Sparta?"

"We grew up together. He's a bit older. He went off and he came back and he was going again but I couldn't go right then so he said for me to meet him. When I went to meet him, he never came."

I couldn't go then because there had been the burial of a family member that I was obliged to attend.

"Doesn't seem like he's very trustworthy, does he?"

I didn't like this slur on my friend's character but let the comment pass.

"I haven't heard anything from him or about him. His family hasn't heard from him. Nobody knows so I don't know whether something happened."

"All right. Let's move forward to where you're twenty-five on the count of three. One . . . two . . . three. Where are you now? Still making sandals?"

"Yes, but I'm married."

"To Shyra?"

"Yes!"

"Mm-hmh! Do you have children?"

"I have one child, a boy."

"What's his name?"

"Luke . . . Luke . . . Luke . . . Lucas."

"Lucas. Mm-hmh! Are you happy?"

"Yes."

"Is Shyra a good wife?"

"Yes."

"And you have a nice home?"

"She's living with us. She lives with my father and myself and my mother and my sister."

In my present mind, I noted the curious order in which I mentioned the members of the family and wondered if it was meant to reflect the hierarchy of respect in the family at that time.

"What did you do, just add a room onto the house?"

"We didn't add a room. The rooms are there."

I was seeing the house, both inside and out, as I spoke of it. It was white-washed, very clean and nice. The walls outside were almost blinding in the bright sunlight but the same walls on the inside offered such dark, cool shade. Windows were holes in the walls. The sandal shop, which was attached to the front of the house, had a big window on the street to let in light onto the tables where we cut and sewed the leather. The window also permitted passersby to chat with us either about such routine subjects as the weather and the health of the family or about particular business at hand. Little more than this was permitted, as my taciturn father didn't encourage idle chatter.

"Do you make a good living making sandals with your father?"

"We do it all together."

The family income was from the sandal shop. Mainly my father and I worked the shop with occasional help from my mother and Shyra. But no one kept track of who made what. Our fortunes rose or fell together.

"Anything else you'd like to tell me? Are you really happy and enjoying life or do you still want to get out for adventure?"

"I don't know about being a soldier but it would be nice to . . . well . . . I think it was my friend that got me interested but now I'm all right being here. It's all right."

"Has he ever come back or have you heard anything?"

"No, nothing."

"All right. Then let's move forward to where you're thirty years of age unless something of importance has happened in between. One . . . two . . . three. Where are you now?"

By now I had received some disturbing news concerning my friend. I was aware, in my present mind, that I was clenching my fists as I lay on the couch and wondered whether or not Tom saw this or sensed a problem from other signs.

"What is wrong?"

"Somebody told me they saw my friend . . ."

"Mm-hmh."

"They saw my friend's head." After a long pause, I said, "Just the head."

"Where was the head? Without any stress or strain now . . . they saw your friend's head?"

"They . . . they . . . he was beheaded. His . . . his head was put on a stake."

"Had he been a robber or a thief or something?"

"No, they just said they saw his head and I . . ." I sighed. "I don't want to believe it."

"Where was this at? In Athens?"

"No."

It was far away that this was reported to have been seen. Usually the farther away the scene of the news the less reliable it was, but these people claimed to have seen it first-hand so it was more likely to be accurate.

"Maybe it's good I didn't go with him."

"Yes. Does your family know this? Or his family?"

"No."

"Are you going to tell them?"

"I'm not sure that I should because I don't know if it's real."

Rather I had no desire to be the bearer of such bad

news and cause a disturbance.

"All right. Anything else you'd like to tell me? Do you have more children than the one?"

"A little girl."

"And what's her name?"

"Shyra, like her mother."

"Is she as beautiful as her mother?"

"I don't think anybody could be as beautiful as her mother."

"You love the mother very much?"

"Well, she's beautiful."

"All right then. On the count of three, let's move forward to where you're thirty-five. One . . . two . . . three. Where are you now?"

"My father died and I'm doing the sandals by myself. Shyra helps and little Lucas helps too. I shouldn't say "little" Lucas because he's actually very helpful.

Lucas was in his early teen years by now and he wasn't little. Somehow in my past-life mind, I had equated "little" with "unhelpful" perhaps as a result of berating from my own father over my shortcomings. Lucas was respectful of me but his respect did not seem to stem from any behavior I exacted from him as much as from Shyra's admirable job of raising him properly.

"Have you heard any more about your friend?"

"No. And I have not said anything to anyone about it. The friend we had in common has gone off again so I've never heard anything more. It seems very much back in the past now. It's just a mystery."

"Maybe in the future we will find the mystery. Then

you're a very happy man with a beautiful wife and a lovely family and a good business?"

"Mm-hmh."

"Let's move forward now until you're forty years of age on the count of three. One . . . two . . . three. Where are you now?"

"I'm still working, living in the same place. My mother's died. Shyra's growing up."

"Is she going to be a beauty like your—"

"Yeah, she is a beautiful girl."

"Is Lucas a nice-looking young man?"

"Mm-hmh. And he helps me. He's a good boy."

I seemed rather blasé about this pleasant life. It certainly didn't seem to be the result of anything I had done. Maybe it was rather what I had not done—not going off to be a soldier—that accounted for it.

"Have you heard anything about your friend?"

"No."

"Has the mutual friend ever come back?"

"No."

"Unless there is something else you'd like to tell me, let's move forward to where you're fifty years of age."

"Not to fifty."

"All right. Let's move forward to where you're forty-five on the count of three. One . . . two . . . three. You're still in Sparta making sandals?"

"Mm-hmh."

"Family's all grown up now?"

"Mm-hmh."

"Is Lucas married?"

"Mm-hmh."

"How 'bout Shyra?"

"No."

"Is she the light of your life?"

"Actually it's Lucas' little boy."

"Ah, your first grandchild. How is your wife Shyra doing?"

"Oh, she's just wonderful."

"Still as beautiful?"

"Yes, and she's a good person."

"Then you're a very happy man, aren't you?"

"Yes."

"Have you heard anything more about your friend?"

"No, but you would think by now he might have come back."

As they got older, people did seem to find their way back home to where they started, or at least this was the case in Sparta.

"I wonder if I had gone with him—maybe what happened wouldn't have—I could have cautioned him."

"Or maybe he would have gotten you into trouble and you would have wound up on the stick."

"That's true. I'm certainly glad I didn't go."

"Yes. You've had a good long life, haven't you? Are you in fairly good health?"

"Yeah."

"All right. Let's move forward to where you're fifty."

"I'm not fifty."

"You're forty-five now, aren't you?"

"I can be forty-eight."

"Are you forty-eight now?"

"I'm forty-eight."

"Then let's move to where you're fifty and see what happens in those two years. You're afraid of them for some reason. Do you know why?"

I wasn't afraid of the years from forty-eight to fifty. I simply knew that I wasn't going to live that long.

"I'm not going to live to fifty."

"All right. Then let's move forward to the last day of your life in this incarnation. You will not have died. You will not have crossed over into spirit. You will feel no pain or emotion. On the count of three. One . . . two . . . three. Where are you now?"

"I'm lying in my bed. Shyra's with me. She's crying. She's knows I'm not going to live long. But . . . "

"Do you have a sickness?"

"Yes."

It was my hands. Little by little they had curled up and become unusable. At first it affected my sandal work until finally I had to stop. Then gradually I became incapable of taking care of myself. My mind was clear but my will to live diminished. The trouble with my hands was the only impediment in a good life so I felt I shouldn't really complain but neither did I want to live.

"Your family is there with you and they're concerned about you but they know you're probably going to die, right?"

"Yes."

"Anything else or shall we take you into the spirit world?"

"That's all. It's been a good life."

"All right. On the count of three without pain or emotion now, I want you to cross over into spirit. One . . . two . . . three. You're now in the spirit world. Where are you in relationship to your physical body? Can you see it and your family?"

"They're carrying my body to a lower room. Shyra's crying." There was a pause and then I continued, "She's good."

It seemed everyone was as reconciled to my death as I was. It had been difficult to take care of me in the end and there was relief as well as genuine sorrow at my passing. Shyra's tears were real tears but also ritual tears. I felt that she could have managed without crying but did so out of loyalty to me and because it was the customary behavior as well, which is why I said that she was good.

She wasn't at all hypocritical. She seemed rather to accept the social order readily and do her part to perpetuate it. There was comfort for me in her always doing so—seeing that things were done right and according to custom. She knew those things and I didn't. On the rare occasion that I paid attention to any required rituals, I quickly forgot them. Without much seeming effort on her part but rather with an easy naturalness, she always did the appropriate thing or displayed the appropriate emotions as she was doing now. It was as if there were no conflict at all between what she knew she should do and what she would choose to do on her own accord. This was certainly not her manner when she was young but seemed to develop with age and became more precious to me as we both grew older. I could rely on her.

"How do you feel?"

"I'm sorry to leave them but I know that everything will be okay. My son will take care of Shyra."

"On the count of three then, I want you to move to where you are with your master again. One . . . two . . . three. Are you with him?"

"Yes."

"Ask him what you were supposed to learn from that lifetime that you reviewed about your friend Clark." Tom paused and then said, "What does he say?"

"He says that the decision I made at the temple made my life go a certain way and he knows that I could see when I was older that it was just as well that I didn't go off with him. That's just the way life works. Sometimes when we're young, we think we know better or we're entranced with somebody else and what they want to do. But we do have our own paths."

"Ask him if there's anything else he has to help you to improve your life."

"He's chuckling again. He says, 'You're enjoying finding this out, aren't you?' and I'm saying, 'Yes,' and he says, 'You do go back a ways, don't you?'"

"Ask him if he has some other lifetimes that you should visit so that you can learn more."

"Yes, he says to go to that very, very early one when I'm ready to do it."

"Okay. Any other lifetimes? Ask him if you've been famous or rich or other special lifetimes that you might visit."

"He says that those aren't too important but if I'm curious, there are those lifetimes as well. He is laughing. He says the best is yet to come."

"In this lifetime?"

"He says this one'll be pretty good. The best is yet to come here but as well down the line."

"Good. Will you thank him for me and for you?"

"Yes."

"All right. I think we had better bring you out of this."

Tom proceeded to guide me out of hypnosis. The immediate effect of this session was mild. There was nothing traumatic, nothing difficult at all. Whatever emotional stressful times there may have been in the course of that lifetime, I didn't re-experience them during the session.

I had asked to see a lifetime in which I had known Clark. This session was the result. Whether or not there have been other past-life connections with him, I don't know. There was no proof that even this one was a genuine past life, whatever that might be, but it did throw some light on the present-life friendship between Clark and me. It seemed that we had a previous life friendship that involved a plan to go off on a soldiering adventure together. He was older, wiser, more manly, more confident than I was in that lifetime. I admired him and wanted to follow him into soldiering. That plan somehow didn't work out, especially for him. My life, although, quieter and less dramatic, seemed more my speed. In the present life, Clark and I were friends. I spoke to him of my ideas about education and he said they were almost identical to Maria Montessori's ideas. Clark was a Montessori teacher and suggested I look into getting trained as a Montessori teacher as well. I did. And then ended up working in the same school with Clark. This time too, friends again, we made a plan (the new school) but circumstances at the time made it difficult to follow through.

One aspect of the present-life friendship was my feeling of obligation towards Clark. It wasn't obsessive, at least not to my way of thinking, but certainly it was strong enough that he could ask me to do almost anything and I wouldn't consider it an imposition. The past life offered reasonable grounds for my feeling of owing something to Clark. My not having gone soldiering with him but having a good life while he had suffered left me with some need to make it up to him. Of course, I wasn't to blame for his failing to show up in Athens at the agreed upon time and place, but my low self-esteem at that time accounted for my feeling at fault. Nor could either of us have predicted the unfolding of our separate lives from that point on. As for whose life was better, that could just be a matter of opinion. The significant point is that, as I perceived it, I let him down.

I told Clark I had done a past-life session in which I found a connection with him. I said I would wait to tell him the details if there was a chance he might try to do a corroborating session himself. After some time, it looked as if he was not all that interested. Instead his initial enthusiasm had just been friendly support for me in my own quest. The details of the past life with Clark did not draw much reaction from him but he responded with interest to the apparent origin of my feeling of obligation. He said it made complete sense. He had become reluctant to ask me for anything anymore as it had become obvious I would hardly ever refuse him. Our friendship had been like that of affectionate siblings, which seemed to me a sufficient explanation for my willingness to do things for him. Until now, I had not really noticed the stronger undercurrent of obligation.

Seeing the past life and discussing it with Clark felt freeing. What was a good friendship could become even better, or so I thought. Instead, to my surprise, the friendship just stopped. The kindly feelings were still there but somehow we just didn't have much contact anymore. Before, we got together often or spoke on the telephone when we weren't actually working together. Now, our contact dwindled to a phone call once every few months. As for the joint project, it stopped altogether.

In this life as before, I had been so charmed by his prowess in his chosen field that I was willing to take on a share in his dreams, this time in the form of our joint business venture. However, with the past-life revelation thrown into the works, I could see that it wasn't my true path that I was embarking on but a borrowed one. It was time to recognize that our paths were parting, to make my way down my own and wish him well on his.

Another issue was the fact that I was a man in this past life. Re-experiencing a life as a man gave me an opportunity to make comparisons about male/female issues. But to begin with, being a male did not feel as dramatically different as I would have expected. When Tom asked if I was male or female, my past-life self answered quite naturally without even the slightest note of astonishment or curiosity registering in my present mind. In that time in Greece, there were clearly defined sexual roles. Man was protector and provider; woman was home-tender. There wasn't any moral judgment about this division of labor along the lines of gender. Neither the man's nor the woman's role was considered better than the other. It was just the accepted norm.

As a young man, I envied my friend for his physical strength, rugged good looks, and his charming personality. By contrast, my physical stature was slight and my self-esteem also diminutive. I didn't have his brawn or brashness, qualities which I deemed essential to the idealized masculine role as soldier. But I found another acceptable male role by following in my father's footsteps.

And I was content with my wife's capability in her female role. I was particularly grateful to her for the maintenance of the details of family life. I stated the rules of the house; she supported them. She knew how to take care of the children. She knew the social rituals and kept them. She seemed to have a feeling for the cycles of life and tended to things as it became time to do so.

I don't know how she came to know these things. Perhaps she learned them from her mother and other older women. Perhaps she learned from her own mistakes as she went along. It seemed natural for a woman to take on these tasks. I was glad she did and did it so well, relieved that I wouldn't be called on to do so myself.

I, in turn, was the provider. I had expertise enough in my profession as sandal-maker. Even though my wife and children helped out, the ultimate burden of keeping up a standard of the work and of making a successful living in the process was on me. This was our family's contribution to the community. It all fitted together like pieces of a puzzle. I had never expected much in that past life but it turned out to be simple and satisfying. I had good, honest work, a beautiful and capable wife, good children, and a place in the community. It was enough. My life was a gradual realization that this could be an equally valid life, perhaps a better one for me than the one that, as a young man, I held out for myself as ideal.

This past life offered several important lessons for me. The lessons were less dramatic than those of the Helvetian past life just experienced but, gently portrayed, the insights were equally important. For one thing, it helped explain the motivations in a present-life relationship. It also gave me the chance to feel what it was like to be a man. And it confirmed the idea that one's life is best lived along one's own path rather than on a borrowed one.

Chapter Eight
A Very Early Life

Fortune had suggested reliving a very old past life. He didn't say why. I certainly had no idea what it would be like but I was curious enough to find out so I arranged to see Tom again. Tom was no longer a stranger. A certain rapport had been established so that we worked together easily. By now I was feeling familiar with the whole process.

The first past-life sessions had been important for me but I was half-decided to make this the last session. As I was not entirely decided about it, I said nothing to Tom about these thoughts when I saw him. He hypnotized me as usual and directed me to Fortune.

"You're now with Fortune. How is he doing?"

"He's sitting there chuckling again. He says, 'You don't give up, do you?' He says that's good. He says there's a lot I can learn from doing this so that's fine."

"Ask him if he has any special message for you."

"He must be very funny today. He's saying he has some message for me but he has to go through his files to find it. But there are no files anywhere around."

"Maybe it's his mental files. Ask him what life you should go back to. He mentioned a very early life. Ask if he can identify it more specifically in order to take you back there."

"He says it's not the very first lifetime on earth but

either the second or third after that. He thinks it's a female lifetime and I don't know more than that."

"All right. On the count of three, I want you to go back to the lifetime that Fortune was talking about, one of your very early lifetimes on this planet. I want you to go back to approximately fifteen years of age. One . . . two . . . three. Where are you now?"

I was having trouble racing so far backwards in time so rapidly. My present mind was just not allowing it to happen. I decided to relax and resign myself to the idea that I could easily go back in a flash what must be thousands of years. As soon as I began to relax into it, images came up. But I didn't trust them. They reminded me of a "caveman" story I had read so I doubted whether they were indeed my own past-life memories. This doubt lingered throughout the session even though none of the particulars of the past life actually matched the specific details of the book I had read.

"Where are you? Can you tell me?"

"It's a forest."

I don't know how these words came out. I seemed to have no part in producing them. Tom continued his questions.

"How is the weather? Is it warm?"

"No. Cold."

Again, strangely, the spoken words seemed to come neither from my present mind or my past life mind, but somehow they came.

"How are you dressed?"

There was a long pause here. Tom tried again.

"Hmm?"

"Something over my shoulder."

"Is it fur or cloth?"

When Tom said "fur or cloth," my present mind seemed capable enough of understanding "fur" and "cloth." My present mind even got busy trying to figure out whether cloth would have been made at this supposedly early period of history or rather pre-history. Yet at the same time, part of me did not make any sense at all of "cloth." My past-life mind was so far removed from my present mind that I could only hear the word as sound, as if someone were clapping cupped hands together. I wasn't paying attention to the meaning, just hearing the sound. And the sound made no sense.

"What is it?"

"Leaves."

I was seeing on myself a garment fashioned of leaves strung together. In my present mind, I figured such a flimsy covering wouldn't offer much protection or last very long. A leaf garment also struck my present mind as a rather corny notion of prehistoric clothing. I was trying to remember what the others wore but had a hard time doing so. I did remember that I had been with other people but I couldn't remember anything about them, even such obvious details as their clothes or their looks.

From the point of view of my present mind looking backwards, it was odd and annoying that I was remembering such an early lifetime perhaps thousands of years ago but couldn't remember, within the confines of that lifetime, from one point of time to another, probably only a matter of days. Tom continued to ask about what I was wearing.

"Is it from a lamb?" There was a pause and then Tom continued. "What seems to be the problem? Do you have difficulty in understanding my questions?"

"It's hard to see."

"Is it night?"

"It's dark."

By "hard to see" I meant that it was difficult to perceive clearly and describe what I was experiencing. The only reason I could think of, after the session, for this difficulty was that I probably wasn't as verbal at such an early period, especially when I hadn't had other people to "talk" with for some time. The gap between my present and past minds was hard to bridge. My guess is that my brain, at that time, was so primitive that my mental faculties were extremely limited.

This apparent difference in brains fascinated me and I thought much about it after the session. But for the time being I was mostly concerned with how I could describe what I was seeing. When I said it was hard to see and Tom asked if it was night, it did then appear to be dark but I wondered whether it was the power of Tom's suggestion or whether I just hadn't noticed the dark before he asked.

"Okay. Let's move forward on the count of three until it is daylight and you are with some other people. One . . . two . . . three. Can you see better now?"

"Mm-hmh."

"Well, what kind of clothes do you have on?"

"Leaves."

"Leaves? Are you male or female?"

"Female."

"Are you with other people?"

"No."

"Do you live with other people?"

"I've lost them."

"Do you know where you are or how to get back to where the others are?"

"No."

"Are you afraid?"

"Yes."

I was struggling to see some people and was disappointed that, even with Tom's suggestion to be with the others, there was no one in sight. In my present mind, I was curious to see who the other people would be. In my past-life mind, I knew I needed to find them to survive. But I couldn't even remember them very well. I didn't seem to have much of a brain to work with. I could look around me, see things, and tell about what I saw but I couldn't do anything requiring more complicated thinking than that.

My present mind wanted to take up the slack by trying to fill in the blanks, look for telltale signs in the environment, explain things, but this other sluggish mind just didn't function very well. Very dimly I recollected other people with whom I belonged, but my efforts to find them were a trial-and-error fumbling along. How I moved was the result of vague wishful thinking rather than of a problem-solving mode of thinking I would adopt if faced with the same situation today.

"The leaves that you wear, how are they made up? Do they cover just parts of you or all of you?"

"They cover my shoulders, come down to my legs. They're all strung together in one piece."

"Does it keep you warm or do you get very cold?"

"Get cold."

"What do you eat?"

"I haven't been eating. I can't find the right . . . the right berries."

"Is that all you eat, berries? Do you kill any animals and eat them?"

"Not often."

"What do you do with the skins? Hmm?"

This all made sense to my present mind but my past-life mind had difficulty answering the questions. I think I probably killed animals when with the other people except that maybe it was only the men who killed animals, the big animals. As for the leaf clothing, I probably fashioned them for myself as an emergency measure because I didn't have tools or skins handy to do otherwise.

"Do you have a name? What do the other people call you? Hmm?"

"They point to me when they want me."

"They don't call you by any name? Do they call anybody by a name? Do you know what I mean by a name?"

My present mind thought, *Of course I know what a name is!* However, I couldn't recollect any name I or anyone else had. It didn't seem very important to my past-life mind, but in my present mind I struggled to find an answer.

"Well, there's the old one. He's lived long."

"And he's the only one that has a name. You call him the Old One, huh?"

It looked as if Tom were struggling right along with me to come up with a name, but in vain.

"And there's his children."

"You are not a child any longer, are you?"

"No."

"Do you have a mate?"

"No."

"Do you want one?"

"No."

That wasn't a crucial issue at this point. What was crucial was my survival.

"Okay. On the count of three I want you to move forward to where you have found the people that you live with, or other people. One . . . two . . . three. Where are you now?"

"Still looking out from the same place, trying to figure out where they are. It's a big hill."

"Are you on top of it?"

"Yes, I'm looking down. I can see far . . . but I can't see them."

"Are there many of them?"

"They're not so many. There's the old one. I don't know."

"Is there one for every one of the fingers that you

have on your hands?"

"Yes."

In my present mind, I knew just what Tom was getting at with this question. He assumed I wouldn't be able to handle numbers in any sophisticated way so he offered the suggestion of counting fingers. Tom's assumption that I couldn't answer the question directly from my past-life mind was correct.

It could also have been that my already limited memory was progressively fading as more time passed since I had last seen them. What memory I did have focused on the old man who represented the security of the group, security that was greatly lacking in my fragile solitary state. It may also have been that my past-life mind was functioning poorly due to starvation. But, in spite of this, I struggled with the numbers questions as well as I could.

"How about the toes on your feet also?"

"Not that many."

"All right. But you're not with anybody. Let's move forward a month from now on the count of three. One . . . two . . . three. Where are you now?"

"Down by the river that I saw from the hill."

"Are you still alone?"

"Yes. I'm going along the river. I know that they were walking along the river."

I noticed that my voice here sounded brighter, more hopeful. Perhaps the river sparked a memory but it wasn't clear if it was the same or some other river.

"Is it a big river or . . . ?"

"Yes."

"Do they have a name for where you live?"

"I don't know."

"Do you get snow there in the—?"

"Yes."

"How do you keep warm when it snows?"

"We stay in the cave."

"Do you know how to get back to your cave?"

"No."

"Is this the first time you've been by yourself?"

"For so long, yes."

"All right. Let's move on down the river and . . . is it morning now? Or is it night? Or what time is it?"

"It's getting dark."

"Do you have to worry about animals killing or attacking you?"

"I think I'm okay by the river."

"All right."

"Maybe if I keep going I'll find them."

"Okay, let's keep going. Let's move forward a week on the count of three. One . . . two . . . three. Are you with your people yet?"

"No. I'm going to go the other way. Maybe they're the other way."

"All right. Let's turn around then."

I heard Tom yawn. Even though I couldn't see him with my eyes closed, I could hear him clearly. I was beginning to wonder if he was getting bored when my attention was suddenly yanked back to the past life. My situation was becoming desperate but I was too tired and weak to be panicky or fearful about my plight.

"It doesn't look familiar."

"Did the other way look familiar at all?"

"More familiar. Kind of like where we were but . . . I don't know which way to go."

"Do you have any idea how old you are? Hmm? Tell me."

"I don't know."

"I see. Are you as grown-up as the women who have children?"

"I don't have children."

"I know you don't but some of the women did have children, didn't they?"

"The older ones."

"Let's move forward a week now on the count of three. One . . . two . . . three. Where are you now?"

I said very weakly, "I can't walk anymore."

"Have you been eating at all?"

"I ate some grass from the side of the river. They looked like the ones we've used before. That's all."

"Have they made you ill? Are you sick?"

"There's just a few. There aren't enough for me."

"Have you found any berries at all?"

"No."

"Are you very hungry?"

"Yes."

"Are you weak?"

"Yes."

"Let's move forward to the next day on the count of three. One . . . two . . . three. What is happening now? Are you still in the same place?"

"My body is."

"Have you passed into spirit?"

"Yes."

"All right. Then you died there on the side of the river?"

"Yes."

"All right. Then on the count of three I want you to move up with Fortune. One . . . two . . . three. You're now with Fortune. Is he still chuckling?"

"No."

"Ask him if he's going through his files."

"He says I would like to know why he wanted me to see a life like that."

"Yeah. Ask him that. What did you learn? What were you supposed to learn?"

"I'm telling him that the only thing is that it seems I need other people. He says, 'Yes, you forget that too often.'"

"Mm-hmh! Then it is a valuable lesson, isn't it?"

"Yes."

"Ask him if he has another message for you now."

"He says not to do any more past-life sessions for a while."

"All right. Ask him if you can go forward into a future life."

"He asks me why I want to do that."

"Ask him if you should, if there'd be something that you could learn that would help you."

"He says you can learn from anything if you want to

but it's not important for me to do that now."

"Ask him if there is anything else we can do at this time."

"He says he can see that I want to know that all this is real and important and there are two ways I can do that. One is to do the verification I talked about. The other is to live for a while with all this that I've been discovering and the truth of it will become apparent. He says it's up to me."

"Ask him if you will be able to contact him when you're not with me."

"He says you will have to show me how."

"That I will?"

"Yes."

"All right, I'll try to. If he will cooperate with you, it'll make it much easier. Ask him if he will do that."

"He says, 'Yes, of course.'"

"Ask him if he will let you know if and when you should do some more past lives in the future."

"He says to take a break."

Usually after being brought out of a past life and re-orienting myself to the present, I would talk with Tom about the session, but this time I didn't feel like talking. I wanted a rest from any more past-life work, including talking about it. Like a turtle, I had stuck my neck out to have a look around all these past lives. Now it was time to pull back into my shell and live with what I had seen for a while by myself.

I had gone into this session intending it to be the last. When Fortune suggested that I take a break, I was grateful for his support of my own decision.

Then I began to wonder again just who Fortune was anyway. If he was a separate entity from myself, had he read my mind and then suggested back to me what I had already decided? Or did he put the idea in my head before the session and then restate it in the course of the session? I wasn't sure that Fortune was anything more than a part of my own mind, in which case it would all just be my own idea anyway. Either way, it was time to call a halt to the past-life sessions.

Meanwhile, this business of Fortune continued to puzzle me. I couldn't figure out who or what he was and now Tom was asking about my contacting him on my own. If Fortune were a real entity separate from me then I figured I would need to be hypnotized in order to make contact. I didn't see how I could talk to him on my own. Nor did I understand why it was necessary. He did seem helpful as a guide through the past-life work and sensible in answering questions on other matters but I saw no reason to seek him out on my own. And if he were just my own inner voice speaking, I didn't need special instructions to talk to myself.

Still, if he was for real, I didn't think it prudent to voice my doubts about him too loudly. I didn't want to court trouble with Fortune just in case he did exist and I didn't want to annoy Tom who seemed to have no trouble believing in Fortune.

Fortune had said there were two ways I could deal with my own doubts about the past-life material. One was to go out and look for some substantiation of the facts.

The other was to live with it all until any inherent truth of it became clear to me. Were these his thoughts or mine? Couldn't I have come up with these simple suggestions on my own? In fact, hadn't I been operating on both of them anyway, sometimes trying to verify data and other times just waiting for it all to make sense eventually? I wanted so much to sort these matters out. I rather liked the idea of a guide I could consult about anything at any time on my own, but I didn't think it made sense to do so based on such flimsy evidence of his existence.

One thing I had noticed was that when Tom directed me to ask questions of Fortune, I didn't have to repeat the questions aloud. I either relied on Fortune's hearing the questions on his own or I just "thought" them to Fortune whether they were Tom's questions or my own. I could see Fortune in my mind's eye as he answered. I didn't actually see his mouth move nor did I hear the sound of his voice in the same way I would normally hear another person's voice speaking. Rather it was the essence of sound that came across in his words and I sensed, without really hearing, the tone of his voice as being low and resonant.

If his response was particularly slow in coming, I discovered that deliberately trying to picture him usually helped the process. Still, when my attention occasionally wandered, the answers would come anyway. As Fortune "thought" his responses to me, I would relay them aloud to Tom. It was clear that the answers did not come from my conscious mind, but whether they came from Fortune as a separate entity or as my inner subconscious mind, I couldn't say for sure.

The next order of business was for Tom to teach me how to contact Fortune on my own. Although I had no plan to use them later, I listened to the instructions. Tom explained that guides could be contacted simply by calling them in one's mind and listening for whatever thought came up as a result. He suggested that in the beginning it was easier to ask only yes or no questions. It was all rather vague and I turned my attention back to the lesson of this past life just seen which seemed simply to be recognizing the need for other people.

I had already wrestled with the issue of people needing other people even to the extent of writing a master's thesis on the subject of loneliness. Now here I was, confronted with the same lesson again. I had negative judgments about people being needy of other people. I saw too much need as weakness whereas self-sufficiency, by contrast, I saw as strength. Maybe I still had more to learn.

I left Tom with a promise to stay in touch. Meanwhile, my decision to pull out of the joint venture with Clark required some tidying up. I catalogued the materials I had collected for the project and turned them all over to him along with any relevant papers. A big hole was opening up in my work life like the Florida sinkholes that were hitting the news at the time. The void soon filled up with a succession of jobs that I was glad to do. As I finished one, another presented itself. A year ended and a new one began open to all possibilities.

Chapter Nine
Interlude: Again with Fortune

The sessions with Tom had stopped, but I continued to read about past lives and reincarnation and mull over my own experiences. I was curious about Fortune and once or twice I tried, somewhat haphazardly, to make contact with him on my own, but I didn't expect much and nothing much happened.

After several months, a friend of mine, whom I had told about the past-life work, became interested in exploring the area himself. In relating my experiences, my own interest was revived so I decided to see Tom again.

Since I had stopped the sessions, I began to notice some stress-related health complaints. I realized that my current uncertainty about work and, more importantly, my intense involvement with the past-life work were aggravating the physical symptoms. But I also knew that the solution was not as simple as securing steady work and forgetting the past-life adventures. Rather it seemed I was on the right track by delving into the past lives, freelance work allowing me the necessary flexibility.

When I saw Tom again, he seemed pleased to see me but was sorry to hear about the physical complaints. He thought Fortune might be able to give some helpful advice about those problems or anything else. I wrote down my concerns and questions and gave them to Tom.

He proceeded to hypnotize me and directed me first to Fortune.

"Ask Fortune if you can have a hug and give him one."

"Yeah, we're doing that. He's saying, 'Did you have a nice vacation?'"

"Tell him we have missed talking to him. What does he say?"

"He says he knows I've been trying to talk to him on my own but you might be able to help me do it more successfully."

"All right. I have some questions that you made out to ask him. Ask if he will cooperate with us in helping you."

"He says, 'Sure, you name it and I'll do it.'"

I had just seen a television presentation of past-life regression in which a complete studio audience was lightly hypnotized and guided through a visualization of past lives, each person to his or her own. The group exercise was an attempt to find for each individual an unusually creative past life that could be drawn upon as a source of creativity for the present lifetime.

Although I was wary of such superficial media presentations, I did find the positive use of past-life regression appealing. Rather than just looking for the causes of problems, one could also look for possible resources to enhance abilities. I told Tom about the television program and about my interest in trying this exercise with him. Tom was willing to ask Fortune about it.

"All right. Ask him if he will help you to tap into any sources of creativity that you have in you and ask him if I'm correct in remembering some previous information he gave us about your real creativity expressing itself in writing."

"He says it is writing—but not the usual kind of writing."

"Ask him to describe it."

"He says that it's not clear because it's not something that has a name. It is work that brings in a lot of different things including writing and designing the way people think about the world . . ."

"I see."

"And it's different. It's not as simple as the butcher, the baker, the candlestick maker."

"Then you're dealing really with intangibles, with a psychic knowledge that can help people to change their lifestyles to learn to live with love."

"He says that I'm not even aware that what I think about is unusual. I assume that everybody thinks the same but they don't. I need to say more about what I think and trust that it's all right."

"Ask him if he will help you to identify what to write and how to write it to get the maximum positive effect."

"He says to write, just to sit down and write whatever comes. Let the quantity come out first and then edit. It will become clear. There's no need to have it perfect before it comes out."

"That's a very wise thing. Do you feel comfortable about doing that?"

"I can try."

"Ask him if he will help you and, as he does so, also take away some of the stress that is causing you to have some physical problems."

"He says what the trouble is is not being patient enough to allow things to reveal themselves and wanting to get on to the next thing too quickly, that there's a big gap that I want to fill, that I want to do things and it's hard to wait. But there's a good reason for it and it's a good exercise in self-discipline. He says to write. Writing and typing. Anytime that I feel a problem or conflict, just write it out. Start writing and keep writing. He's putting this picture in front of me. It is papers and papers and papers full of writing. And he says, 'You get the idea?'"

Fortune put before me a visual image of papers all filled up with words just endlessly piling up and then blowing all over. The pages kept on being produced so fast that there was no time for any order to establish itself. Words, words, and more words!

"Do you understand now what he means? Write it down, utilize it if you can. If not, you've learned something in the process and you've also gotten rid of a lot of the stress, the anger and the other frustration in your life, isn't that true?"

Tom's interpretation of the message wasn't quite correct. Fortune wasn't suggesting I do writing as therapy to rid myself of negative emotions. In fact, it was very important that the writing be without any purpose whatsoever, at least at first. The point was just to fill pages with words. However, I didn't want to divert my attention from Fortune's message by disagreeing with Tom who obviously only wanted to help.

"He says, 'Do the writing. Just write.' I should just start writing. He says, 'Try to get over the blocks and judgments about writing that it's going to be useless and all that. Just do it.'"

"All right. Ask him which lifetime would be of the most value for you to go back to right now."

"He says to send me through the tunnel and you'll find out."

"All right. That we will do."

Chapter Ten
As Pieter, the German Calligrapher

"Now I am ready to regress you back into a previous lifetime that Fortune wants us to go to. I want you to step into the tunnel that'll take you back to your own past life. Tell me when you're in the tunnel."

"I'm there."

"All right. I'm going to count backwards from five to one and on the count of one you will find yourself at the age of fifteen in this other lifetime we are now going to re-visit."

As Tom continued with the instructions for the time tunnel routine, I was also remembering an image of a clock on which the hands spun backwards extremely fast.

"Number one. You are now there. Where are you? Are you indoors or are you out-of-doors?"

"I'm indoors."

I had just entered a large stone building through two huge wooden doors. The doors slammed behind me with an echo as I stepped cautiously into the building and gazed about me. The building was like a church but not a church. The ceilings were very high and I felt very small. I was awestruck at the size of the building and also at my being there. I wasn't supposed to be there. I had passed by this building many times but I hadn't gone in before even though I had wanted to.

"All right. Tell me about yourself. What is your

name?"

"Hans."

"Hans? What's your last name?"

"Dopfel."

"Okay. Where do you live?"

"It's Germany."

"And what year is it?"

"I don't know."

"All right. On the count of three, you will know what the year is. One . . . two . . . three. What year is it?"

"16 . . . something."

"16 . . . what? You will remember. It'll become very clear to you now. One . . . two . . . three."

"1617."

"1617. Do you live in the city?"

"Small town."

"What's the name of the town?"

"Starts with M. Mainz. Mainz. Mainz."

"All right. What is the nearest big city to you?"

"It's pretty big."

"Is it Frankfurt on Mainz?"

"Oh no."

"Is it a suburb of the city of Frankfurt?"

"It's not . . ."

"It's what?" The word "suburb" made no sense to my past mind.

"Hmm? Well, that's all right. Let it go for now. On the count of three, you will know exactly where you live and where it is and identify it. One . . . two . . . three."

"It's Mainz and it's a castle town and it's high on the

hill and I'm in the castle now."

"I see."

"I'm looking at the stones."

"Speak louder, please."

"I'm wearing leather pants. Short leather pants."

They were grey and had suspenders. After being asked to speak louder, I thought maybe I should also speak more, so I volunteered the information about the clothes perhaps after having been asked about my clothes in previous sessions.

"Do you live in the castle? Is that where your family lives?"

"No."

"Or do you work there?"

"Visiting."

"Who are you visiting? Is it the prince that lives in the castle or his family?"

I had the feeling that this building may have been a castle at one time but was not being used as such now or it would have been considerably more difficult for me to have gained entrance. Even so, the people in charge wouldn't have liked my being there nor would my family.

"Actually I'm not supposed to be here."

"Did you sneak in with some of the servants?"

"I just went in by myself to look. I wanted to see."

I was looking for something specific. The building was large and imposing and therefore important, I thought. What I was looking for was important, at least to me, so this seemed a good place to look, but I didn't see any evidence that this was the special place I was looking for.

"It's not so special."

"Is your family wealthy?"

"No."

"Are they very poor?"

"No."

"Do you have brothers and sisters?"

"An older brother. I have a younger sister."

"I see. Are you a happy child?"

I was slightly annoyed with these questions about my family, as I would have preferred to talk about the building and what I was looking for. With the question about being happy, I realized there were at least two ways I could answer—either for the moment, which was more frustrated than happy, or for my life in general, which was how I chose to answer.

"Yes."

"Do you go to school?"

"I don't know about that."

"All right. On the count of three you will know whether you go to school and what you are studying. One . . . two . . . three. Do you go to school or are you an apprentice to something?"

The word "apprentice" made sense to my past mind but not the word "school." Learning to me meant apprenticeship, either formal or informal, the latter being what my older brother was doing with my father which meant helping out and learning the trade. The formal apprenticeship (usually with someone outside the immediate family) was what I wanted to do. I wanted to learn about making books.

"I want to be an apprentice."

"I see. What does your father do? Is he a tradesman?"

"He does business. He sells things and my brother does that with him."

"But you don't want to do it?"

"No."

"What do you want to do?"

"I want to see where they make the books."

"Mm-hmh!"

"I know they do."

I had been dissuaded from this interest by my family, primarily my father, but it remained a secret wish of mine.

"Do they make books in the castle?"

"No. I don't know. I was thinking maybe they did but no, I don't think they do."

"All right. Anything else you'd like to tell me or shall we move forward to the next important event in your life?"

"There's something nice about the stones. The streets have the stones in them and the castle has big stones. The stones feel so nice."

"Do you think you would like to work with the stones as a stone mason or as a sculptor?"

"People cut in the stones."

"Mm-hmh."

"They cut in the stones and I wonder about that. I'd like to do that but I like the stones and I wonder if it hurts the stones. I don't tell anybody that. Sounds funny."

"You're a very sensitive person. Do you have many friends or do you spend most of the time by yourself?"

"I have some friends, but they're silly."

"And you're a very serious person?"

"I guess."

"Do you love animals and enjoy the woods and the fields?"

"You have to go down to the woods. The town is so high."

The castle sat at the edge of the town that overlooked the river. It was possible to see east across the river to the trees and fields way down on the other side. The town itself was so built up that there were few, if any, trees in the main part of the town and certainly not right in the square that the castle fronted on. The castle may have been a church.

"Are you living in the mountains?"

"No, it's just the town is high."

"Okay. Shall we move forward then to the next important event in your life? On the count of three then. One . . . two . . . three. Where are you now? Are you still in your hometown?"

"Yes. I'm in the house. I'm looking out the window. I can see below in the streets there's a big clamor. There's something going on."

"How old are you now?"

"Oh . . . sixteen."

"Do you know if it's a riot or what's going on?"

"Somebody's coming and I don't know who it is, but everybody's cheering and . . . they're coming in a cart."

"Who is coming? Describe them to me."

"They're pulling a cart up the long stone road. They're pulling it into the square. We live down the street from the square and I can just see a little bit into the square. I can't tell what's happening. I want to go down and find out."

From the second-floor balcony of our house, I could see between and beyond the buildings on the opposite side of the street to the long stone road leading out of the town. A frenzied crowd was approaching from that direction. People were spilling out of the buildings in town and converging on the central square to see what was happening.

"My mother says it's dangerous. It's not good to go amongst those people."

"Ask her what is happening. She must know."

"She says I don't need to know. I should not involve myself with those people. They're dangerous. They're not . . . I shouldn't go."

"Do you go?"

There was a long pause and then I spoke very quietly. "Yes."

"And what happens?"

"They've thrown the person from the cart. They're beating him. I don't know what he's done."

"Do you know who it is?"

"I don't know who it is. It's a man."

"Is there anybody there that you can ask?"

"No, I don't want anyone to see me. I'm afraid they'll tell my mother."

"Do you want to get away from there now?"

"I don't . . . I don't know what it's about. It is scary."

"All right."

"But I don't know . . . I can't tell what the people are saying. They seem to be excited and watching. Why are they watching? I don't know why they are watching. I don't know why they don't stop beating him."

"What are they beating him with?"

"They're beating him with sticks and with their hands."

"Is he on the ground now?"

"Yes, he's on the stones."

I was thinking "those beautiful stones."

"Is he bleeding?"

"Yes."

"Does the man die?"

"He's not even doing anything. He's letting them beat him. I don't know what it's all about. It stopped."

"And the man is still alive?"

"Yes. The people are going."

"They're leaving?"

"They think he's dead."

"They think he's dead?"

"Yes."

"Do you think he's alive?"

"Yes. I want to help him."

"Do you help him?"

"I want to wait until everybody goes. I don't want anybody to see me."

"All right. On the count of three, let's move forward

'til everybody is gone. One . . . two . . . three. Everybody is now gone. Do you help the man up and take him to your house? Or what?"

"Oh. I wish it would get dark. Then I could do something and nobody would see. He's still lying on the street. I can see him from where I am."

My position was just at the corner where a side street led into the main square. There was a well of some sort in the middle of the square that obstructed my view of the beaten man lying on the other side of the square. After this session, I noted that I had said "lying on the street" rather than "lying in the street"—a grammatical construction that was strange to me but clearly not just a slip of the tongue.

"I'm afraid. I don't know whether I should go home or whether I should help him, but he's saying something."

My first impulse was to help whomever it was as he was badly hurt and obviously needed help. I could understand no reason why he should have the beating and be left to die. Still, I wasn't supposed to be there and without fully understanding the situation, I might be getting in way over my head by attempting to help.

"All right. On the count of three, we will move ahead until it is dark and you will either have helped him or gone home. One . . . two . . . three. Tell me what happens."

"I know that he wants me to help him and I know he's saying it's okay if I wait until after dark. I know it in his head he's saying that to me. I don't know how I know that."

"It's all right. You're getting it psychically."

"He knows I'm afraid and he says it's all right if I just wait and then come to him."

"Is it getting dark now?"

"Yes. I'm going to him. It feels like I know him. It feels like . . ." I gasped, "Ooooohhhhhh!"

"Without any trauma now, without any stress . . . "

"I didn't know. It's my father!"

"Oh, Lord! But that's all right. Without any stress or strain now, pick him up and take him wherever you want to. Are you going to take him home?"

"I don't think my mother knows."

"Can you lift him up? Are you strong enough to lift him up?"

Throughout this dialogue, I was crying.

"Yes. You know what he says?"

"What?"

"He says to leave him on the stones. He says to leave him there, that the stones are okay, they feel good. I didn't know he thought that too."

This was a great moment for me as I had never before felt that he was my real father or that I was a part of the family. His comment about the stones opened a line of connection with him that was an unexpected treasure in the midst of the anguish.

"I can't leave him on the stones though."

I had been sighing through much of this past life so far, almost at every statement as if the world were too much with me. I was, in today's slang, a "space cadet," more comfortable in the world of mind than the world of matter. Reading people's minds came easily to me. What was amazing here was that for that length of time since he had been brought into town until I recognized him and even while I was reading his thoughts, I didn't seem to realize that it was my father. Perhaps it was an example of denial—the psychological mechanism that protects one from an unpleasant truth for as long as possible.

"Okay. Let's move forward an hour and you tell me what you have done. One . . . two . . . three."

"I have to take him home. I'm taking him home. I'm almost there."

"Let's move forward to where you are in the house. What does your mother do?"

"She's not there."

"Do you take him up to bed?"

"No. There's a bench in the hall. I put him on the bench. I don't know what to do next."

I was on the ground floor of the house. The bench was just inside the front door on the left. It was a heavy wooden bench and easily long enough to accommodate my father. There was no noise from the upper floor. The house was deserted.

"Do you clean him up and wipe the blood off?"

"Yes, but mostly I just stay with him. I don't know where my mother is gone. He's asleep or maybe . . . no, he's still alive. He's breathing but I don't know what this is all about."

"Is it warm out or should you cover him up?"

"Yes, uh, he needs some blankets."

"All right. Get some blankets on him and let him sleep."

With this question, my mind leaped from that past life to the present. I wondered if, without Tom's prompting, I would have looked for blankets. I may well have just continued to sit there trying to make sense of things rather than dealing with the immediate physical demands of the situation.

"Is there a doctor around that you can call?"

I hesitated at this suggestion because I figured if all these people were willing to stand by to see my father beaten to death without lifting a finger, where would I find someone, even a doctor, who would be inclined to help? Also, for some reason, I felt I needed to know why he was beaten before I sought any authorities, medical or otherwise.

"I don't want to leave him. I can't figure out—"

"Is he awake at all? Can you talk to him?"

"No."

Tom kept making practical suggestions while I, in my past life, sat stupefied by the situation.

"All right."

"I don't know what's going to happen when the daylight comes. I don't know where my mother is and I don't know where my sister is. The house is empty. They left. There's food on the table. They left the food sitting there."

"The food is?"

"Yes. They must have left in a hurry."

"Were they taken?"

"I don't know. I don't think so."

"All right. Let's move forward in time now to the next

day on the count of three. One . . . two . . . three. What is happening now?"

"My brother is come."

The strange grammatical construction here—"is come" instead of "has come"—occurred several times throughout this past life. I wondered if this was an exact translation of the language of the time and place because it certainly was not my present way of speaking.

"He said I should come with him, that I should leave my father there and come with him."

"Ask him why. What did your father do?"

"He said he won't tell me but I should not be with him. I should leave him there and come with my mother and my sister and him. They're staying at some other people's house and I should come with him there. My mother is very upset with me for going off. I asked my brother if she knows about my helping my father. He says, 'Don't say anything, just come.' And he's very upset too. He doesn't even want to look at my father. I don't know why he doesn't want to look at him, but he's leaving him."

"Tell him you won't leave until he tells you what your father is done or what is wrong."

The strange form of grammar—"is done"—must be contagious! Was Tom picking it up by telepathy?

"I already said that. I don't want to go. It's my father. I want to stay with him."

My wanting to stay with my father was not due to altruism on my part but due to guilt for having disappointed him in life whereas my brother had done as he had wished by following in his footsteps. Now the situation was reversed. My brother wanted nothing to do with him and I found myself, silently and desperately, promising my father to do as he wished, even if it meant abandoning my great desire to make books if only he lived.

"All right. Let's move forward."

"He's dead."

"Your father is dead?"

"Yes."

"All right. Then there's really no reason to stay, is there? He's stopped breathing?"

All I could do here was sigh. Tom chose to move on through the life.

"Now, without any stress, strain, or trauma, and simply as though you were an observer: are you going to go to your mother now?"

"No."

"Are you going to stay there?"

"No."

"What are you going to do?"

"I'm just going to go. I'm going to go down the road. I don't know where to go. I'm just going to walk."

"You're going to leave home now for good?"

"Yes. I don't know what to do, but I'm going to go down the road."

"Did you find out what your father did?"

"No."

"Okay. Let's move forward then. Are you ready now to move forward to the next important event in your life?"

"I'm packing everything up and I'm going to go."

"All right. Let's move forward to where you have everything packed and you are leaving. Is there anyone around to see you?"

"No, I'm going by myself."

"Is there anybody on the streets or do the neighbors know you're leaving?"

"I'm sneaking out."

"Out the back way?"

"I'm covering my head and nobody can see who it is. I'm walking by myself and I have packed a little food and bread and I'm going down a long stone road. I'm tired, but I'm going."

My present mind thought it unwise to start off on any such journey while so exhausted emotionally. But my past-life self thought it wise to get away as quickly as possible from what I couldn't understand. I could always try to catch sleep wherever I could later.

"Okay. On the count of three, let's move forward to the next day. One . . . two . . . three. Where are you now?"

"I'm beside the road. I hear people going by back and forth on the road but not very often. I hid down the side of the road for the night and I slept well but now . . . I don't know. It seems like the whole world has changed. There's the big road and I have to go on it now. I know I should go on it. I can't go back now but oh . . . I don't know. There are people talking."

"What are they talking of?"

"I think they may be talking about my mother and my brother and my sister."

"What are they saying about them?"

"I'm not sure it's about them, but they're talking about some people and they're saying that they came and took those people away—a woman and a daughter and a son. They don't tell the names. I don't know if it's my mother. I have a feeling it is."

"What did they say the reason for it was?"

"They said that it's . . . they didn't say the reason but they said it's on account of my father."

"What had your father done?"

"They don't say. I don't know if it's good they took them, or bad. I don't know. I don't know where they're going to take them to. I guess I can't go back now."

"No, they'd take you then, wouldn't they?"

"Yes."

"Was it soldiers that took them or police?"

"Like soldiers."

"Mm-hmh."

"Oh, I wish I knew what was going on." I sighed deeply.

"Okay. On the count of three, let's move forward another day One . . . two . . . three. Where are you now?"

"I'm walking and I'm thinking that I should have a whole new story, that I shouldn't say my old name and that I should give myself a new name so that nobody knows who I am. And I'm thinking about what that story should be. I'm thinking about it but I don't know what to say."

"All right. Let's move forward a week on the count of three. One . . . two . . . three. Where are you now?"

"I'm coming into a farm. I started to tell them my

story and they didn't want to hear it. They just said, 'Well, if you want some work and you want something to eat, then you better come work at our farm.' I thought that was okay, so I'm coming to work at their farm."

"What is your name now?"

"Pieter."

"Pieter what?"

"Oh, I didn't think of another name."

"Well, you had better think of one quick."

"I'll take their name."

"What is their name?"

"I don't know but I'll just take whatever theirs is. I'll say mine's the same."

"All right. Let's move forward then three months and see what happens on the count of three without any stress or strain. One . . . two . . . three. What are you doing now?"

"Well, I'm working at the farm, but in fact you know what happened?"

"What?"

"I took their name. Their name is Voss. I'm Pieter Voss. When I said my name was Voss, they thought I must be a relative so they were very happy to have me there but it's just that I took their name."

"Do you get along well with them?"

"Yeah, it's okay."

"Do they have any children?"

"Yeah."

"Do you get along well with them?"

"Yeah." Then I said quietly, "They have a daughter."

"A pretty one."

"Mm-hmh."

"You have your eye on her?"

"Yeah."

"Is she friendly to you?"

"Yes. She looks at me and winks."

I was picturing her amongst the others at haying time. She was being coy around the ladder that leaned against the hay wagon. We were all working together but she was very playful and just to tease me she wouldn't work near me for too long at a time.

"Let's move forward to the next important event in your life on the count of three. One . . . two . . . three. Where are you now?"

"I'm in a big, b-i-i-g church."

"What are you doing there? How old are you?"

"Twenty."

"Are you a member of the church or a priest or a minister or what?"

"I suppose you could say I'm the oldest of the boys, the boys that sing in the choir. I'm still doing that. Most of them are younger than me."

"I see. Do you still live with the Vosses?"

"Oh no."

"What do you do now?"

"In this church they have somebody that does the writing."

"And what do you want to do? Do you want to learn that?"

"Yeah, I'm learning it."

"Are you good at it?"

"He says I am."

"What type of writing do you do? Calligraphy?"

"Yes, well . . . I do some of the decoration. I have to learn the stories so that I know how to do the decoration right, so the pictures are right."

"Are you able to read now?"

"They read the stories to us."

"Are you learning to read also?"

"No."

"Have you ever learned what happened to your family?"

"No, and I don't want to talk about it." This was said in a whisper.

"I see. Is the town where you were born and raised far away from where you are now? What city are you living in incidentally?"

"I should know that."

My present mind was speaking here.

"All right. On the count of three you will know what city you're in. One . . . two . . . three. What city is it?"

"I will tell you the name when I learn to write it."

"Well, let me know." Tom waited a while and then asked, "What is it?"

"I haven't learned to write it yet."

"Oh, you haven't. Well, ask somebody to tell it to you so you can tell me."

"Something like Bitburg."

"All right. You are now learning how to write, draw and make pictures. Do you draw the pictures too?"

"That's all I do because I don't know how to do the writing."

"Do you use colors or do you—"

"Yes."

"Then you're an artist?"

"Well, I use the . . . I fill in the colors."

"I see. Does somebody sketch out the form first?"

"Yes."

"Do you enjoy this type of thing?"

"Yes."

"Do you have any . . . are you married?"

"No."

"Do you have any girlfriends?"

"No."

"Do you have any boyfriends? Friends that you spend any time with or do you live totally by yourself?"

"Well, there are these other boys that are in the choir and I have to be friends with them. I should be nice to them but I stay pretty much by myself."

"Where do you live? Do you live in the church or do you have a room some place or where do you eat?"

"I help take care of the animals and I usually just sleep with them in the barn. It's next to the church."

"What do they have? Horses? Cows?"

"They have a few little things for the people in the church. Some sheep and some goats and some pigs and chickens."

"Do you eat well?"

"Yeah."

"All right. Anything else you'd like to tell me?"

"No."

"Shall we move forward?"

"Okay."

"On the count of three, I want you to move forward to the next important event in your life. One . . . two . . . three. Where are you now?"

"I'm sitting on the stool and I'm doing the writing. And I do it very well."

"Is that calligraphic writing?"

"Yes, it's very beautiful. I try to make it very, very, very beautiful."

"Mm-hmh! How old are you now?"

"Oh, twenty-five."

"Do you still sleep in the barn? Or do you have a place of your own or what?"

"I have a room. There's a room in the church where I stay. It's not where I do my work but it's nearby. And I wonder why. It seems funny that I'm here now. I thought . . . I don't know. It's what I want to do but I'm surprised that I'm able to do it."

"Have you ever learned anything about your family?"

"No, I can't find out unless somebody just happens to tell me because if I ask . . . well, it's a mystery."

Considering that I took very little interest in worldly affairs, my inquiry might arouse suspicion as to my relationship to the family and I might find myself in danger as well. I decided to avoid the whole issue.

"Have you ever gone back to your hometown?"

"No. But I'd like to."

I was still interested in seeing how they made the

books.

"Are you happier now?"

"Yes."

"Where do you eat? Do you do your own cooking? Do you eat with other people in restaurants or at their home or what? How do you eat?"

"There are some women in the church who cook for the people in the church and I'm one of the people in the church. When I was taking care of the animals, I would sometimes be involved with that but now I do the writing all the time and I just go for my meals. I don't do anything about it."

"I see. Do you draw pictures now as well as color them in or do you just write?"

"I'm not doing the pictures now. I'm just doing the writing."

"Are you the only one doing the writing?"

"Well, I do most of it."

"Are you able to read now?"

"Yes, of course."

"What town is this? Can you tell me what the name of the town is now?"

"Rheims."

"What city is that near? Are you still in Germany?"

"I don't know if it's Germany."

"Is somebody there with you? Ask them if they know where you are—what country you are in. What do they say? On the count of three, you will know what the city is. One . . . two . . . three."

"Rheims."

"And the country?"

"France."

"France. Is that Rennes in France or Rheims?"

"Rheims."

"That's the way it's pronounced. It is spelled R-E-N-N-E-S."

I wasn't seeing that spelling. I knew it was Rheims but I didn't feel like contradicting.

"Do you work in the big cathedral in Rennes?"

"I do the writing."

"Mm-hmh! And it's in that big beautiful cathedral that's in Rennes?"

"Yes."

"What do you do when you're not working? Do you have a girlfriend?"

"No."

"You're not in the choir. Do you have any friends at all?"

"Yes, I have friends, but . . . they're not . . . living."

"Now explain that, if you would."

"When I'm not doing the writing, I go into the church."

"Mm-hmh."

"And I kneel down."

"Mm-hmh."

"And my friends talk to me. They're not living people. They're voices."

"Will you ask them what has happened to your family? Ask them if they are alive. Go into the church now. On the count of three I want you in the church kneeling down talking to your friends and ask them what is happened to your family. One . . . two . . . three."

I did not like the way I was being told what to do and resented being asked to use my friends, but in my past-life mind I assumed that whoever was making this request probably meant well even if he lacked respect and sensitivity. So I complied.

"They say my family is dead. They say it was the wrong family for me, that I have found my right family, that I'm doing my work and . . . I should be happy with that."

None of this was news to me as I had already surmised my family was dead, a family I never had felt part of anyway.

"Was the Voss family your right family?"

"No, no. They're my right family."

I was referring to the friends I talked to as voices.

"Oh, they are. I see."

"I have a bigger family than a family on earth. I'm doing my work and I'm on the earth but I was only born into that family. That wasn't my real family."

"Did you ever ask them what your father did that was so wrong that he and the rest of your family were killed?"

"They said that if I know that I will be disturbed and it won't help. I should just carry on with my work. It doesn't concern me."

"Okay. On the count of three, without any stress or strain, let's move on to the next important even in your life. One . . . two . . . three. Where are you now and what are you doing?"

"Oh, I'm working so hard."

"Doing the same thing?"

"Yes."

"Are you still in Rennes?"

I wished he would get the name of the city—Rheims—right, but even so I didn't correct him.

"Yes, but you see, people have come from so far. They know my work now and they come and they want me to have me do some work for them. I'm so good at it."

"Do you still use the name Pieter Voss?"

"I don't use Voss. They just call me Pieter."

"Do you participate in any of the church ceremonies?"

"No."

"What is so important about what is going on now that you are so famous for your beautiful calligraphy?"

"Well, you see, one of the people that came was an old man and this old man said he knows me. He says that I don't have any secrets from him. He knows that my name isn't Pieter, that I was born with a different name but that I was very wise to choose the name Pieter. He says the rock that the church stands on is Peter and that my work is helping the church to stand so it's very good that I took the name Pieter. He says it just shows that I'm on the right path. I don't know why this man tells me all this but it sounds very right. I'm scared that he knows me so well because I think he must know about my father but then I'm realizing maybe he doesn't know about that. He just has some information. He can know things like I know things so it's nice to meet somebody like him."

I was referring to knowing things through intuition rather than through spoken discourse.

"All right. Are you still single or are you married?"

"I'm not going to marry."

"You're not going to marry? Are you a celibate?"

"Yes."

"Do you know the name of the church that you work in?"

"It's Pieter's." I was chuckling as I said this.

"St. Peter's?"

"No, not St. Peter's. It's Pieter's church."

"Is it a Catholic church?"

"Yes."

"Is it that beautiful cathedral in Rennes?"

"It's very beautiful and it's very tall and it's got beautiful stone and the stones are nice here, too. I like the stones."

"Mm-hmh!"

"And I like my room where I work and I like my work and sometimes I'm so full of such a wonderful feeling doing my work. Sometimes I think it'll just burst the stones!"

This simple statement barely conveys the overwhelming rush of feeling here. I felt infused with the Holy Spirit to the extent that I was one with it, with everything. It was absolutely glorious. Although I had asked to tap into a positive creative experience in a past life, this—the ultimate source of creativity in divine inspiration—was more than I had bargained for.

"You're a very fortunate person, aren't you?"

"Do you know why they call it Pieter's church?"

"No."

"Because it's me, they call it Pieter's church."

"I see. What . . . what is its—"

"Because of my work."

"What is its other name? What was the name it originally had?"

"Well, it's just the church. It's the only one."

All this talk about the church being named after me was just my own concoction. The experience of divine inspiration may have fed some latent delusions of grandeur, which in themselves probably resulted from living so removed from the world.

"All right. On the count of three, I want you to move forward to the next very important event in your life. One . . . two . . . three. Where are you now?"

"There's some commotion outside. I don't know what it is. Something is going on. I'm going out to check. It's night and it's dark and I can't see. My eyes are very bad. My eyes can't see. I think it's from working so close all the time."

"How old are you now?"

"Sixty-five."

"Mm-hmh! Have you stayed there in the church all the time working?"

"Yes."

"Been very happy?"

"Yes."

"Do you still see your friend that knew about you or

is he died?"

"He's gone. He came only that one time. He stayed a while and then he said from then on he will only send me messages. He's done that. He was true."

"How is your health other than your eyes?"

"Good."

"All right. Let's move forward in time to where you're outside and tell me what's happening out there."

"There are some horses coming."

"Is there a war on at this time?"

"I don't concern myself with anything in the world."

"Mm-hmh."

"But there are horses coming. There are horses and there are people and there are lights. There are candles and they're coming through the streets. They're going every which way and I'm going out to see. Oooooooooohhhhhhh!"

"What happened?"

"I'm knocked down."

"By a horse?"

"No, by the people. They're just running and crowding. I fell down."

The candles were large torches of fire. People were running through the night with them. There was such a commotion that it was impossible to make sense of it. I was reminded of the time my father was brought into town on a cart and beaten to death except it was daylight then and everyone seemed to know what was happening (even if I didn't) and tacitly allowed it to take place. But this was general panic. Everybody was running and screaming through the streets. No one seemed to know what was going on or why.

It was rather unusual for me even to bother about what went on in the world outside of my writing, but I thought I had better check on this disturbance. I was just outside the church when I was knocked down. The horses and crowd were coming into the square from the street opposite the church, mixing in the square and then moving down the streets on either side of the church.

"Do you get up?"

"No. They're gone." This was said weakly.

"The people are gone?"

"The people are gone."

"All right. Are you still lying on the ground?"

"Yes . . . my head."

"Are you dying?"

"Oh, I can't be dying from just that."

"All right. Let's move forward to the next day then if you're still alive. On the count of three, One . . . two . . . three. Where are you now? Are you still at the church?"

"I'm on the street. I'm lying down. My head hurts. Ooh, my head."

"Does somebody come and rescue you?"

"Yes."

"From the church?"

"No. A small boy."

"And he takes you home?"

"No, he's too little."

"Is it daylight now?"

"No, it's night. He shouldn't be out."

"Can you get up?"

"No. Well, maybe I can."

"Yeah, try getting up."

I tried very slowly to pull myself up from the stones. My head hurt again as soon as I moved but I was distracted enough by the little boy that I didn't feel the pain too keenly.

"He says he knows me. He says he knows I'm the one that does the writing. He says he wants to learn the writing."

"But you don't know what happened?"

"No."

"When I was lying on the stones, I remembered my father."

"Yes, it's a duplicate of it."

"I remembered my father and how he was lying on the stones and the boy coming to help me this time. He's not my son."

"No."

"But he wants to learn the writing."

"All right. Let's move forward to the next day then. One . . . two . . . three. What has happened?"

"I've gone back into the room and I'm doing the writing and the boy has disappeared. I don't know who he is and he didn't tell me his name. I wanted to find him because he wanted to learn the writing and also I'd like him to come and help me. I need some help."

"Well, tell the people around there to look for him. Describe him. I'm sure they'll find him."

I lived too cloistered a life to function well in the

world beyond the walls of the church. My inability to make practical decisions evoked Tom's desire to be of help. He kept offering advice or specific directives, such as he was doing here. But my present mind found this troublesome.

I understood the past-life regression as a re-living of a memory of what had already happened. Tom shouldn't be able to tell me what to do but only ask what came next. If, in the past life, I did as he told me to do, it could only be that he had just happened to anticipate the next action correctly. Otherwise his directives seemed to violate the rules of chronological sequence. Perhaps, I considered, there was no real past being remembered but only a directed fantasy all happening in the present. Or, that time was a much more fluid thing than I realized, that what we think of as separate times can flow back and forth into each other. As my present mind was occupied with these thoughts, the past life continued.

"I'm going into the church. I'm going to see what my friends say."

"All right. What are they telling you?"

"They're saying I don't have long to live, that a boy will come again."

"Will you live long enough to teach him?"

"They say I should start to teach him the writing."

"Ask them what you were supposed to learn in this life." Tom waited before asking, "What do they say?"

"They say I can't really be asking that question."

"All right. Ask them what I should be learning."

My mind split on this question. My present mind

thought, *Yes, how clever to take advantage of this apparent source of wisdom*, but my past mind couldn't make any sense of the question at all.

"What?"

"What do they say?"

"Someone's coming."

I was in the main part of the church where I always went to consult my spirit friends. I'm not sure if I really heard someone coming through the door just then or whether I was looking for a plausible excuse to avoid further questions in this vein.

"Is that the boy?"

"No. No. I wish I had told him I would teach him but my head was hurting so much when he asked that I didn't want to talk."

"Well, your friends just told you that he will come so don't worry about it. Did you ask them what I should be learning in my present incarnation?"

"I don't understand."

"All right. Then let it go. Let's move forward in time to the next important event in your life. One . . . two . . . three. Where are you now? Are you still in the church? Still writing?"

"Yes."

"Is the boy with you?"

"No."

"What is happening that's important?"

"People are going. They're all going."

"Where are they going?"

"Everyone's leaving the town."

"Is there a plague? Ask them why they're leaving."

"Something bad's coming. Something very, very, very bad."

"Is there an invading army?"

"They said the devil's work is coming."

"Okay. Let's move forward until whatever is going to happen in the town happens. One . . . two . . . three. First of all, do you stay?"

"Yes."

"Okay. What is happening now?"

"The boy is come."

"He didn't run away, did he?"

"He's come to get me. He says I should go with everybody."

"Do you go?"

"I said I'm too old to go. I'll stay and do my writing. He's going."

"All right. Let's move forward then."

At this point, I kept sighing, something it seems I did a lot in this lifetime. Tom continued.

"What has happened?"

"I'm so weak."

"Are you still in the church?"

"Yes."

"Is there an army come, or some illness?"

"Nobody's come, nothing's come. I'm there by myself."

"You're the only person in the town?"

"I think so. I'll go to the door." I went to the door and looked out. "It doesn't seem anybody's here."

"Are you very ill now?"

"I'm not ill but I can't . . . They took the food with them. They took the animals, they took everything."

"And you're starving?"

"Yes."

"All right. On the count of three, I want you to move forward to the next important event in your life and it may be the last day of your life. One . . . two . . . three. Where are you now?"

All of a sudden, I cried out, "My friends!"

"Hmm? Without any stress or strain now, I want you to let go of everything, simply as though you were an observer. Are you with your friends that you talk to in the church?"

"They're not talking. They're not there. I don't know what to do. I came to find out what to do . . ." Here my voice became weak and talking took a great deal of effort.

"And I . . . they're not there. They've gone, too!"

"Are you very weak now?"

"Yes."

"Is this the last day of your life?"

"Yes."

"All right. Now remember you will not have died. You will not have crossed over into spirit but it will be the last day of your life. Now as an absolute command, you will feel no pain or emotion but re-experience this situation only as an observer. One . . . two . . . three. Where are you now?"

"I'm with my friends."

"You're still alive though?"

"No."

"Oh, have you died?"

"My body's down there on the stones."

"I see. And you're looking down at it?"

"Mm-hmh."

"How do you feel now? Do you feel happy?"

"Yes."

"Do you feel that you did what you were supposed to do in this life?"

"I didn't teach the boy."

"That's all right. You've kept the memory of how to do that into this present incarnation, didn't you? That's why you are so proficient in it now."

"Oh, I'm looking at my body on the stones."

I wasn't ready yet for philosophizing. I was still too near having died to conjecture about the meaning of that life or this present one.

"All right. Shall we move, go back with Fortune? On the count of three. One . . . two . . . three. How's Fortune? Is he still sitting on his rock?"

"Yes. Now he's getting up and coming to me. He's giving me a hug. He says, 'We both love stones and rocks, don't we?' And I'm laughing and he's laughing. Fortune says, 'As I have told you, you must do the writing.'"

"Mm-hmh! That is your life now, isn't it?"

"He says it's not writing like I did before but that I ought to start writing."

"Ask him if there's another lifetime we should go back to right now or soon."

"He says this one has been good and the few

216

months' break showed me I need to assimilate things as I go. There's more to learn but I can do it another time. He says just to take a little bit at a time and it's fine. I'm doing fine, he says. And that's it. He's going to go sit on his rock."

"Thank him very much."

Tom proceeded with the usual gentle exit routine. When I came out of the hypnotic state, I felt as if I were teetering on the brink between two different worlds, past and present. I was fascinated by my spacey other-worldly orientation as Pieter, the celibate calligrapher. I felt surprisingly at ease in that persona.

The session touched on many different issues. There was the moment of inspiration as a calligrapher that was sheer ecstasy—the pure joy of inspired creative work. A glory suffused everything. It was in me, yes, but not contained by me. It would be more accurate to say that I was in it, a part of it, and the work was a part of it too. The feeling was grand.

The session, indeed all of the sessions, were worth doing for that one experience of divine spirit, a spirit so powerful that even massive stone walls could not contain it. To have known that feeling and to be able to remember it was and will continue to be a treasure. I had asked to tap sources of creativity and the source was divine. Hard work and sacrifices of comfort were also required but the reward was so great by comparison. To be able to create, to be an embodiment of God in the world was the greatest pleasure imaginable and it resulted in beautiful work.

What struck me long after the session was what happened immediately after I experienced this grand infusion of the spirit. I quickly lapsed into an egotistical banter about the church being named after me. The church wasn't named after me at all but I was just trying to claim all this glory for my own. Of course, to claim that all-pervasive spirit as mine and mine alone was a sacrilege that brought it all down very quickly from something grand to something merely grandiose. That in itself was a lesson.

Such inspiration is only viable when it is allowed to flow through a person, not stopped up in order to aggrandize oneself by it. If one is blessed with it, it cannot be contained but must be allowed to move through and on. By its very nature it expands, reaches out, permeates. Here was my own experience of that ancient truth.

Then I became curious to know, assuming that past life had really occurred, whether I had experienced that incredible event the same way in that life itself as I did now upon re-living it? Maybe it didn't really matter because even if it didn't happen just like that at the time, it did happen somehow for me now. The experience was real and valid in substance. Here was another valuable lesson. To fuss over the mechanics of the process was a way of not appreciating the gift of spiritual knowledge gained by such an experience.

Chapter Eleven
Interlude: Fortune's Directive

The message was certainly strong and clear that I should write. But what? I had often thought about being a writer. But my image of a writer was someone with something burning inside that just had to be written. Where was that burning in me? And what I should write about?

I was convinced that if I forced myself to write without a subject, whatever it was, the result would be a disaster. I saw bookstores filled from floor to ceiling with words. Surely I had no business adding more unless I had something worth contributing.

With this directive from Fortune to write, I thought about my relationship to books. Books—what a marvelous way to pass along thought and learning and entertainment. And just as strongly I have despised books, seeing them as self-righteous little things puffing themselves up out of all proportion to their minimal importance, especially compared with real hands-on living in the world. Of course, not all books are the same.

And I knew book learning wasn't everything in life. Once, in a perverse mood, I imagined a delectable happening: that in a single moment everything written on paper would dissolve. People would have to depend on themselves and each other instead of books.

Here now I was confronted with an order to write. I tried. I sat down and tried to write . . . anything. I wrote as if writing a diary. Soon my writing took the form of remonstrance against Fortune who had directed me to this task in the first place. As much doubt as I had, it is a wonder that I continued. For not only did I have doubts, but my uncertainty and confusion about the whole adventure threw me into a rotten abyss of gloom. And insanity was probably lurking somewhere in that black pit. Was I to trust this strange new form of guidance?

I continued to rage against this command to write. Fortune was responsible for setting me to this task, so naturally my ranting and raving were aimed at him. To my surprise, Fortune answered.

The writing turned into a dialogue with Fortune. I would ask a question, and type it out. Then I would find myself typing out an answer that presumably came from Fortune. This developed so gradually that it was some time before I noticed that what I was doing might be called channeling, in this case channeling Fortune's replies.

It was such a subtle form of transmission. No big trumpets or neon signs. No audible or visible confirmation of Fortune's answering or speaking to me. I doubted Fortune's answers were anything but my own. Yet there was a definite felt presence of him and a consistent tone and quality to his answers, which were different from the character of my questions. Our voices were different. And the answers kept coming.

I continued to write. I was instructed by Fortune not to look at what I wrote. If I were to stop and read, I would start judging, criticizing, and probably call a halt to the whole undertaking. I was merely to write, it didn't matter what, just to fill up page after page with words. So this was how I began this new assignment but it was a faltering start, like the wobbly first steps of a baby.

On the other hand, I was already doing another kind of writing. From the very first past-life session, the Mexican lifetime, I had been transcribing the recordings after each session. This process allowed a more thorough examination of each past life. As I listened to Tom's questions and my answers, I could easily drop back into any life and remember the details clearly. There were parts that were unavoidably emotional and gave me chills whenever I heard them again. But for the most part, I tried to focus just on getting the words down right.

I realized that any recording was already one step removed from the past-life experience itself. It retained the tone of voice and pace of speech but there was so much I remembered that was not in the recorded dialogue. So I decided to add descriptive and explanatory comments to put some flesh on the bones of the skeleton dialogue.

I had thought I was finished with all the past-life stuff but stopping for a few months was not the end, just a temporary break. And a fruitful break at that, for with renewed vigor I tackled the transcribing. And I decided to see Tom again. Among the people in my present life I had asked about a past-life connection with was my mother. My mother and I had what I assumed was a usual mother-daughter relationship—close but with the occasional probably inevitable disagreement.

He hypnotized me and turned on the recorder at the

end of his usual induction routine.

"On the count of three, I want you to join your guide your friend, your good buddy and see if he's still sitting on his rock. One . . . two . . . three. What has he got to say today?"

"He's still in the rock."

"Is he smiling? Is he happy?"

"Can't see him in the rock."

"Oh, I see. Well, on the count of three, he will show himself. One . . . two . . . three. Can you see him now?"

In the beginning, I had discounted the whole guide business. I would have said it was Tom who was leading me through the sessions. Indeed, he was in charge of the step-by-step process but it was Fortune who was the ultimate guidance, whoever Fortune was. And yet here now Tom was commanding Fortune to appear. It seemed rather brazen of Tom, the earthly helper, to expect Fortune, the so-called spirit guide, to jump to his one-two-threes. But the thought passed with the moment and we moved right along.

"Yes, I can see him."

"What's he doing?"

"He says he's feeling lazy. He doesn't want to have to work."

Tom laughed heartily at this but I continued.

"He likes it in his rock."

"I see. Well, tell him you won't bother him too much today."

"He says he doesn't want to do much work today. He says I can do the work."

"Good. Ask him if he is satisfied with your progress."

"He says yes."

"Has he been satisfied with your daily communications with him?"

"There haven't been daily communications."

"Would you commit yourself now to start it?"

"Sure."

Having finished the transcribing, I was planning to continue more seriously with the other writing I had already started.

When I met Tom this time, I told him I was ready to do whatever seemed best. As usual, he deferred to Fortune. "Let's put you under and see what Fortune thinks you should do," he said. I didn't particularly like the phrase "put you under." It brought to mind an image of a bully maliciously forcing some defenseless child under water. But I wasn't interested in dwelling on such an image or improving on the choice of words. I was interested in being hypnotized and seeing what Fortune would have to say.

Fortune was still puzzling to me. I couldn't figure out just who or what he was. Was he my conscience? Was he inside me, outside me, or both? Tom thought Fortune was an entity complete unto himself and always acquiesced to any instructions from him. But I thought Fortune might very well be just another construct of my imagination like the past lives had seemed to be.

Tom hypnotized me and directed me to Fortune. The rest of the session was an extended conversation with Fortune dealing with topics such as my work and my future. I was so interested in what Fortune had to say that the time sped by even faster than it usually did while under hypnosis. Fortune dealt with so many questions and so thoroughly that I hardly had anything to say to Tom after the session. I thanked him, took the recording home and then discovered nothing had been recorded.

When I saw Tom again, I told him about the blank recording. Undaunted by the loss of the last session, we began another one. Tom induced hypnosis and I relaxed into it very easily.

"On the count of three, I want you to meet Fortune. One . . . two . . . three. How's Fortune doing today?"

"He's there. Says hello."

"Tell Fortune that I send my best wishes. Ask him if he is finding it easier to communicate with you."

"He says it's easier and there are times when it can go quite freely. He says there's another issue, which is that I get too personally wrapped up in things. If only I could just allow things to move through me and consider myself as a vessel and not judge so quickly, things will move more easily. He says I want to be right. That's true, I know. He says the point for me to remember is that rightness doesn't attach to me personally. If I leave myself out of it, rightness is there. It needs more trust in something bigger."

"Mm-hmh."

"He says the idea is to write and to leave myself out of it, just to write."

"Well, thank him very much, will you?"

"He points at me and says, 'Write! Write! Write!' He's

laughing."

"Tell him I enjoy his laughter. Now what should we do for you?"

"He knows I'm curious about a past-life connection with my mother. But he says it's not important to do that now. He says I should be writing. 'Go home and write,' he says."

"Ask him if it's all right, since you're now in trance and we'd like to experiment, to try cutting out your conscious mind completely during a session, perhaps in a past life with your mother."

I had read of the novelist Taylor Caldwell's past-life sessions in which she went so deeply into the hypnotic state that she couldn't remember any of it afterwards. I wondered whether this meant that during the session itself she was not given a post-hypnotic suggestion to remember everything afterwards or whether her conscious mind did not monitor the past-life experience while it was going on. I hadn't been hypnotized so deeply but Tom had said people can be hypnotized more quickly and deeply with each succeeding session.

I wanted to try being hypnotized deeply enough to lose temporarily that part of my mind that kept intruding on my past-life experience. I figured that if the present conscious mind could be kept at bay, what came up from the past would be untampered with, and therefore more reliably accurate. Tom had agreed to see what could be done.

"Fortune says it won't work to cut out my conscious mind. He says what will help is when I start pulling myself back from the writing and allow things to come through me. He said when I get to that stage, I can do a past life without my analyzing it. He suggests waiting until then to do one about my mother. He says it won't work now."

"Is there anything else we can do now?"

"He says I have to trust that I'm doing okay. He says when I start writing that I shouldn't look at anything I've written but just keep writing. After I get to a point, a lot of what he's saying will become very clear. He says, 'When you're doing the writing, do the dialogue. That'll work.'"

It was about this time that my first harangues had evolved into a sort of dialogue with Fortune in which I constantly challenged his edict to write as well as his very existence.

"And he says, 'Remember this isn't going to be pretty, this writing. Pretty writing is your hobby now, not your work. He says he needs to pull back now and go to his rock. He says I'm becoming . . . he's seeping into me . . . I'm becoming a rock . . . and . . . he needs to go back to his rock and pull back."

"Tell him thank you very much. I shall look forward to our next visit."

Tom must have proceeded then to bring me back out of hypnosis but I was not at all aware of it because a very strange thing happened just then which caught my complete attention. I felt as if Fortune and his rock were one and the same thing and I was merging to become one with that thing as well. I felt as if I were opening up in an acceptance of Fortune and as I did so, he seeped into me, an infusion of his essence as a rock. It was as if his rock molecules were intermingling with my molecules so that I became harder and harder as the proportion of rock molecules to my molecules increased. The feeling was pleasant at first. I was utterly intrigued by this unexpected and bizarre happening. Part of me sat back and watched the show while the rest of me slowly turned into a rock.

Then it seemed the rock was taking over all of me including the part that was just watching. I became afraid of losing myself entirely. Just as the panic of fear set in, Fortune said he needed to pull back, and did so. Little by little, the process reversed itself. The rock-hardness dissolved gradually. I was able to differentiate between myself and Fortune again. I was my old familiar self and he was his familiar self, recognizable in his leathers and feathers.

This was the most compelling part of the session. Tom brought me quickly out of the hypnosis. I emerged breathless with wonder about the meaning of it all. I tried to describe to Tom what had happened but my description must have been rather garbled. He couldn't make much sense of it.

Later on in my own written conversations with Fortune, I asked him about this occurrence. Fortune responded that it was an experience of allowing myself to be an instrument, a vehicle, a channel. He advised me to study what happened. He suggested that it was another way of understanding the process of channeling. I had always imagined that one was still oneself while allowing whatever it was to pass through oneself much like ink flows through a pen. Instead, it was possible one could lose one's self-awareness entirely and become something completely different and not necessarily something of fluid material either but possibly something as hard as a rock. Spirit could manifest in any form.

I had experienced the fear of losing myself as it was happening but as soon as I became afraid, Fortune had pulled back and let me be. He didn't force the issue. His stern demeanor was complimented by a kind and gentle forbearance. For me to continue would have required more trust than I was able to muster at that point. But the lesson, as far as it went, was not wasted. It gave me new respect for Fortune—his wisdom, his way of teaching, and his compassion.

Chapter Twelve
As Orcus in Old Jerusalem

I had made a good beginning in my dialogue with Fortune. I amassed a sizable stack of papers filled with words. And I did not look back to read any of it. Mechanically, it was easy to type out the conversations with Fortune. It was only when I stopped long enough to think about what I was doing that problems arose, mainly problems of believability. What came through from Fortune during a hypnosis session was more believable, if only slightly, than what I was doing on my own. I figured that my conscious mind was less of an obstacle when I was hypnotized than when I was just writing by myself. After working at the dialogues for some time, I wanted to be hypnotized again, not necessarily to re-experience a past life but just to compare the difference in modes of consciousness. I arranged to see Tom again.

During the first sessions, Tom had directed me to Fortune after reliving the past lives. But subsequent sessions had begun with Fortune who then suggested how to proceed. This time too, Tom hypnotized me and directed me first to Fortune.

"I want you to let go of all of your Earthly connections now and meet your guide, Fortune. One ... two ... three. How's Fortune doing today?"

"He's there and he says hello to you."

"Good. I send my best wishes. Ask Fortune if he

would show himself to you so that you can see him clearly."

Whenever I contacted Fortune on my own, I didn't really see him clearly. However, if I chose to focus on his looks, details were immediately apparent. It was as if he sat in my peripheral vision and whenever I chose to turn my head and look directly at him, I could catch a good glimpse. It seemed that the message was more important than in what form it came. So I was not in the habit of dwelling on Fortune's looks. But now in my mind's eye, I turned my attention to his appearance.

"I can see him, more clearly now. He says it's not necessary to see him this clearly when I'm writing."

"Good."

"He says that the trip I went on was important, as he already told me, because I need to learn how to do both the walking and the writing when I'm not in a familiar place. I'll be traveling and I need to get into the practice. That was a trial run. He says, 'Not too bad.'"

I had gone on a short trip to Santa Fe, New Mexico to visit my sister. The visit had allowed some time for quiet walks and writing on my own.

"All right. Do you want to go back to a lifetime now with your mother?"

"Yes."

"On the count of three. One . . . two . . . three. Where are you now? Are you indoors or are you out-of-doors? What is happening?"

"Fortune is still there. He's being funny. He's jumping up and down and alternating his feet. He's doing a funny little dance. Now he's serious again. He says he's going to his rock, but he says that when we go to a past life, go through the tunnel gradually. It's hard for me to do it fast."

Tom proceeded with the tunnel routine and at the end, as I stepped out of the tunnel, Tom asked again where I was.

"Outdoors. Very, very bright."

"Are you standing in sunlight?"

"Yes. It's very hot."

"Are you in a city? Or out in the country?"

"It's between buildings. The buildings are all painted white. The sun is very bright and it's very hot."

I was standing in a street that wasn't a constructed street but just a space between the houses. As such, it did not go straight but found its way by zigzagging between the buildings. The buildings were one-story houses or small shops that were quite close to each other some of them having walls in common and others having alleys between them. The houses appeared to be made of clay or clay bricks and had rounded corners. The rounded corners gave the structures a soft look but the mid-day light reflecting off their white-washed walls was hard on the eyes. The light and heat made me thirsty. Even answering the questions was difficult with my parched lips.

"The sun is reflecting off the buildings on you, huh?"

"Yes."

"What country are you in?"

"It's Jerusalem."

The buildings reminded me of the adobe houses in Santa Fe, New Mexico where I had just been visiting. I had a fleeting thought that it was Santa Fe but the thought passed as quickly as I was aware of it. When Tom asked what country I was in, there was no hesitation in saying the name. It didn't even bother me that Jerusalem was the name of a city, not a country.

"Jerusalem. And what year is it?"

"I don't know."

"On the count of three, you will know. One . . . two . . . three. What year is it?"

"2."

"2 A.D.?"

"Yes."

This logically did not make sense but Tom did not challenge it. Many of the dates did not feel as firm as other parts of the past-life reporting. I was not sure why but it may have been because the dates were not important in the past lives. But then I couldn't be sure who it was answering the questions about dates.

"All right. And are you fifteen years of age?"

"Yes."

"Are you male or female?"

"Female."

"Do you live in either one of these houses that you're standing in between?"

"No. I live a ways away. It's on a hill."

"I see. What are you doing there?"

I was remembering my house as seen coming from town. It wasn't a big hill or a big house but the position of the house just on the crest of the hill and next to a shady tree silhouetted it dramatically against the sky. When Tom asked what I was doing, I had to think for a minute whether he meant at the house or in town where I was at the moment. I realized he meant the latter.

"I'm lost."

"You're lost? Are you a long distance from your home?"

"No, I'm not really lost. I think I know where I am. But I haven't been in this part of the town before. The houses are not familiar."

"Do you live in a big house? Is your family wealthy?"

"No, it's a small house."

"What is your name?"

"Orcus."

"Orcus? How would you spell it, do you think? O-r-c-a-s. Does that sound about right?"

"Maybe."

O-r-c-u-s seemed the better spelling to my present mind but I let it be. What Tom suggested was close enough.

"All right. What do you do? Do you work or do you just stay at home or what?"

"I mend things."

"Clothes or other things?"

"Clothes."

"What are you doing? Are you delivering some clothes to somebody or why are you in this strange section of town?"

"I just wanted to walk this way."

"On the count of three, I want you back close to your home again. One . . . two . . . three. Where are you now?"

"I'm walking out of this part of town and I'm walking up the hill and it's stony and—" I sighed.

"Hmm?"

"I'm carrying my sandal 'cause it broke."

"I see. Are the rocks hurting your feet?"

"I'm going slowly so they don't hurt. I don't have to hurry. It's too hot to hurry. I'm going in the house. We have a big jar, a jug of water by the door. It's very cool."

"Are you drinking a lot of it?"

"Yes."

"Is your mother there?"

"Nobody's here."

If anyone else had been there, I would not have drunk so much water. Although the large pot was more than half full, the water, a precious commodity, had to last a long time.

"Do you live with your mother and father or do you live alone?"

"I was living with everybody but they've gone on a trip. I'm here by myself."

"But that's just temporarily."

"Yes."

"What's your mother and father's name?"

"Susa."

"Is that your mother?"

"Yeah."

"What's your father's name?"

"I don't know my father."

"Doesn't he live there with you?"

"The man that lives with my mother isn't my father."

"I see. Was your father killed or what happened to your father?"

"I don't know. I never knew him. My mother doesn't talk about him."

"I see. What is the name of the man that lives with your mother?"

"Frankus."

"Is he nice to you?"

"He doesn't pay much attention to me."

"Are you an attractive young lady?"

"Yes."

Frankus tended to ignore me because he was a little frightened of me. My mother and I were very close so he dared not anger her by having a bad relationship with me. Occasionally, he would joke with me or scold me slightly but there wasn't much strong feeling expressed in either case.

"Do you have brothers and sisters?"

"Not really. They're their children."

"So they're your half-brothers."

"Yeah."

"You're the oldest?"

"Right."

"Do you get along well with the children?"

"Yes."

"How many of them are there?"

"Three."

"What are their names?"

"Corinna."

"And what are the others?"

"The other ones are having new names. They're going to get new names."

"I see. What does the man do that lives there in the house with your mother?"

"I don't think he does anything."

"Does your mother work?"

"Yes, she does mending too. He doesn't walk very well."

"How was he injured? Or was he born that way?"

"Yes. He has a funny foot."

"What we, in this life, would call a club foot?"

"It turns around funny. It's shorter than the other one so he wobbles when he walks. He's a bit mean on account of it."

"Does he beat your mother or you or the other children?"

"He's not very kind to her. She's very nice to him but he doesn't deserve it really."

This was not a serious complaint on my part and I didn't intend to do anything about it. My policy with him was to live and let live. He didn't bother me; I didn't bother him.

"Where have they gone on a trip now?"

"They've taken the children. They're going to get some new names."

"Where do they get the new names from?"

"I don't understand. They go somewhere, do some ceremony and they get new names."

"What race or religion are you?"

"It doesn't really have a name."

"You're not Hebrew?"

"Most of the people are."

"But are you?"

"No."

"And are you living in Jerusalem now?"

"Outside of it."

"All right. Anything else you'd like to tell me?"

"My mother doesn't believe what all the other people believe. That's one reason we live so far. And she thinks . . . she talks to . . . I don't think I want to tell you."

"Please tell me. What does your mother talk about and how is she different? Is she a Christian?"

"I don't think I better tell."

"You can tell it. It will be safe with me. I will not tell anybody else in Jerusalem. I promise."

"She talks to trees and she talks to rocks. She talks to different kinds of things in the world. People think she's strange."

"Mm-hmh."

"But she doesn't do all that they think she does. They don't know much about her. They just think she's strange."

"Does she have any special powers?"

"I don't think I'd better talk about it."

As my present self, I was eager to hear more about these beliefs and practices and peeved at my past self's reluctance to speak. I sensed that Tom was annoyed too but with his usual patience he carried on.

"Please talk about it. It's important that you do and I told you I will never tell anybody in Jerusalem where you live there in that incarnation."

Tom's promise was juggled back and forth between my past and present minds and seemed to pass inspection.

"She can heal!"

"Mm-hmh!"

"She thinks she can heal this man's foot. But she hasn't been able to."

"Did she ever go to Nazareth or did she know what we call Jesus Christ and his wanderings and his teaching? Or did you see him?"

"She talks about something like that."

"All right. Is that your mother in your present incarnation?"

"No."

"Do you know at this time who your mother from your present incarnation is in that lifetime?"

"This man with the foot."

"The man with the foot is your mother in this present incarnation?"

"Yes."

"Can you talk louder? You're not speaking very loud."

"I'm afraid to tell you these things."

"Well, don't be afraid. I guarantee you that they will never be passed on to anybody in Jerusalem or any place else in that incarnation that you're now examining. You are perfectly safe. And it is important that you talk about it."

"I'm worrying about it. I don't know what to think. I'm concerned about when they come back because my mother thinks that if they go to this place—it's some place where there's water, some spring near a tree—and she wants to give the children new names there and she thinks that if my f-f—well, not my father but she wants me to call him my father—he doesn't like all this that she does but he likes her and it's funny how they are."

There was much that could be said about the relationship between my stepfather and mother but I left most of it to them to deal with and only concentrated on the difference between their beliefs. My stepfather was willing to go to my mother's sacred place because he was interested in being healed. Ordinarily, he considered my mother's beliefs nonsense but going to her sacred place to try to be healed could work in his favor whatever the outcome. If he went and was cured, then he had that to look forward to. If he wasn't cured, at least he could tell my mother "I told you so" about her unusual beliefs. My mother told him that if he were to take another name, the cure would probably be surer but he wouldn't go along with that. She said the next best thing then was for his children to be given new names. He did agree to that. While they were gone, I imagined some other possible outcomes of the expedition. I figured my stepfather might get very angry if he weren't cured or get angry if he were cured and therefore proven wrong in his own beliefs. I was anxious about the whole project.

"She wants to cure him. She thinks maybe if he goes

with her there that his foot can be cured. I'm afraid. I don't know what will happen."

"All right. Just relax now without any emotion. What's he going to do with the other children? Have them baptized?"

"No."

"What does water have to do with their getting new names?"

Tom may have been thinking about the Christian rite of baptism, which was not the case here. Perhaps the Christian practice of cleansing the body with water to symbolize purification of the soul derived from this older water ritual, a ritual central to my mother's beliefs.

"All right. On the count of three then, let's move forward to where they have been there and come back. One . . . two . . . three. You're all back in the house and your mother will describe what happened. How is everybody?"

"They're fine. They got new names. That was okay."

"Were they put in the water when they got new names?"

"No."

"Was water sprinkled on them when they got new names?"

"No. I don't think so."

"Ask your mother what they did when they got the names."

"She says that I can't know that. I would have to go with her. She says if I don't want to learn from her, I shouldn't ask her questions."

"Was the man you call your father's foot healed?"

"No. And he's hurting because it was a long walk. And he's angry. He says it's good I'm not learning those things from her because it's not right. It's old and it's stupid."

"Ask her if she believes in Jesus Christ."

"She says what she knows is right."

"Just ask her what she believes in. What religion does she believe in?"

"She says these are things you don't say. They're names that you use at the time. She can't even say the two names of the children—the two new names. She has to wait until she knows that it's all right to say them. She knows them. She's got them but she's still calling them by their old names. They don't have any old names. She just calls them 'boy' and 'girl.' She says you're not to give them names until they have their true names."

"All right. Any other questions you want to ask her?"

"I am not quite sure what to believe. I don't really understand. I love my mother but her ways are strange. They were fine when I was younger. The other children don't seem to mind. They're so small. But I don't know who to believe. You see, if he had come back and his foot was okay, then I know that my mother was right but it isn't and so I don't know what to believe."

"All right."

"I'm doing my mending but I can't stop thinking about it. Sometimes I just wish his foot would get better. I think he wouldn't be so mean."

"Does he still beat you?"

"He's just angry. He shouts. He shouts so that it hurts."

"Does he ever do anything to you physically?"

"Just shouts."

"Doesn't lay his hands on you?"

"He did once."

"What did he do?"

"He tried to grab me but I ran away and he can't run fast with his foot like that. So I always stay far from him."

"How old are you now?"

"About seventeen."

"They were gone a long time when they were getting the names changed?"

"No, not so long."

"Anything else you'd like to tell me or shall we move forward to where you're twenty and see what happens? On the count of three, then. One . . . two . . . three. Where are you now?"

"I'm trying to find the place that they went to."

"What? Did your family leave?"

"No. I'm trying to find out about this. I want to find out why she believes this. Nobody else believes it. He says it's old and it doesn't work and she should stop believing it. I can't find the place. She told me where to go but I can't find it."

"On the count of three you will have found it. One . . . two . . . three. You're now at the place with the spring. What is it like?"

"It's beautiful."

"Is there anybody there?"

"It's all shaded. All of the trees grow so thick and they hang over and the water comes down. The trees are wonderful. It's as if the trees and the water just love each other."

The tone of my voice changed as I described the mysterious place. It was a miracle in itself how this gushing spring could burst forth in the midst of extremely arid country. There was a rocky outcropping, a mound of rocks covered by trees. The water came out of the top of the rocks and cascaded down into a shady pool. The water was refreshing and the shade a welcome respite from the merciless heat.

"There's such a nice feeling here. It's shady and it's cool. And you can put your feet in the water and it's cool."

"And it's hot otherwise?"

"Yes."

"All right. Ask the water or whatever voice it is that gives names to describe to you what is happening so that you learn about them."

My present mind was thinking how silly and yet creative of Tom to try to ask the water to talk. My past mind had no problem with the idea but I didn't know how to go about it.

"I don't know how to talk to it."

"Just mentally think as if you're talking aloud. Say that you came here because of your mother, to learn what she knows."

"I know that, but she wouldn't help me. She said that I'm coming here to disprove her so she wouldn't tell me how to do it. I don't know."

"Try it."

"She said there's a name that you call but she wouldn't tell me the name. She said I only want to prove her wrong. That's not the spirit to go in. But it feels so nice here."

"Well just say, 'I don't know your name but please talk to me so that I will understand you' and see what happens. What happens?"

"I'm just staying by the side."

"Now do you know what you should do?"

"I have a feeling."

"You have a feeling?"

"It must be very quiet. Can't talk."

I was hoping that Tom wouldn't say anything because it was clear to me that there had to be absolute silence, but . . .

"Well, you can talk to me 'cause they cannot hear you."

"Ah! Nobody can talk."

Just then there seemed to well up in the trees and rocks and water and air a certain essence of each of them that blended together and swirled around. It grew greater than the forms it came from so that they were subordinate to it. My past mind was very involved in what was happening. Yet my present mind was vaguely aware that Tom was turning the recorder off during long silences. Then it no longer mattered that he stay quiet as I was drawn into the past beyond the influence of any interruptions from the present, or my present mind.

"And the tree is coming out of the tree and the rocks

are there and the rocks are coming out of the rocks. I don't understand and I'm frightened."

At this point, it was as if my own essence were being drawn out of me to blend with the big swirling of light that was wonderful and entrancing but also fearful as I was becoming lost in it.

"Now, without any emotion now. Something is going to happen."

Something already was happening! Tom's words brought me back to my present mind just enough to recognize this as a mystical experience and to wonder about the meaning of it but the experience itself was too overwhelming to stand back from it and reflect on it just then.

"Oooooooooohhhhh!"

"On the count of three, move forward now to where things have happened and you understand. One . . . two . . . three. What is happening now?"

"I'm running away."

"You said that the water was coming out of the water and the trees were coming out of the trees and the rocks out of the rocks?"

"Oh, I don't know. I don't understand it. I'm running. I don't know. I'm going back."

"Where are you going back to?"

"I don't know. I don't want to go back to that place."

"Don't you think you should go to get the answer?"

"I'm too frightened."

"All right. On the count of three, you will not be frightened anymore. One . . . two . . . three. Now all the fear is gone. You're curious. You want to go back."

Certainly my present mind was curious but the mind of the past prevailed.

"I can't go back now. I'm going to go back to the town. Maybe I'll come another time."

"Okay. What is happening now? Are you with your parents again? Your mother?"

"No. I'm in town and I'm going to a friend. I'm going to this family. I do the mending for that family . . . I've come to them. I've told them I can't go back to my mother. They said that's good, that she's very strange and that I shouldn't go back there. They said I could stay with them."

"How old are you now?"

"I'm twenty."

"Have you been interested in any boys or young men?"

"That's one reason I came to this family."

"The young man that's there?"

"Yes."

"Is he your lover?"

"Oh no."

"Your friend?"

"Well, I like him and he likes me but his family is afraid about me so they don't want me to be very friendly with him because of my mother and her strange ways. I haven't told them where I have just come from."

I might have tried to ingratiate myself by saying I had gone to the sacred shrine in order to disprove my mother's beliefs. But in so doing I would have transgressed the loyalty of daughter to mother, however strange the mother might be. Besides, I wouldn't be very convincing if I said I thought it all nonsense because I was ambivalent myself. There was certainly something very powerful at that place. There may have been more to my mother's beliefs than I or anyone else had allowed. But I had enough of a burden to bear as my mother's daughter without broadcasting an interest of my own on the matter. I figured the wisest course was to say nothing at all.

"I said I was just away. They said I can stay if I do the mending and help around the house. But I shouldn't go off with the son by myself."

"All right. On the count of three, I want you to move to where you are twenty-one years of age. One . . . two . . . three. Where are you now?"

"I'm going to find where he's gone."

"Who? The young man?"

"Yes."

"Let's move forward then, on the count of three, to where you've found him. One . . . two . . . three. Where are you now?"

"He's with a group of other men. I don't want to go too near."

"What are they doing?"

"They're talking and they're laughing. They're sitting under some trees. I don't know what they're talking and laughing about. It's so hard to see him. It's so hard to be with him. He likes me but he doesn't want to anger his parents."

"What do you want to do?"

"They have another woman for him to marry."

Arranged marriage was the usual form of marriage. Even in those rare cases where there was an instance of choosing one's own mate, the semblance of parental arrangement was still important. In this case, his family was of a higher social position than my own so it was not going to be possible for me to marry this young man.

"Let's move forward then to where the group is breaking up, on the count of three. One . . . two . . . three. Did you hear what they were talking and laughing about?"

I didn't really care. All I was there for was to see this man. I didn't want to interrupt the group. A woman wouldn't do that, especially one who was something of an outcast. I didn't want to cause any trouble for this man because he might turn against me completely. The friendship, such as it was, rested on a fragile base. I had no desire to hear the conversation anyway. As men's talk, it didn't really interest me.

"He saw me and he's going the other way. He's a little frightened of me too but he likes me. I think he thinks I'm like my mother. He's not sure whether he should have anything to do with me. This has been going on for so long. I think he's going to marry the other person."

"All right. Let's move forward to where you're twenty-two on the count of three. One . . . two . . . three. What is happening now? Are you still with the family?"

"Yes."

"Is he married?"

"Yes."

"Have you ever seen your mother since you went to that spring?"

"No."

"Are you going to go back?"

"Well, I did see her but she didn't see me. She came into town once."

"Are you happy now?"

"No."

"Do you miss your mother?"

"I'm angry."

My present mind was surprised that Tom let slip the comment that I was angry without any further questions.

"How about your father? Have you seen him?"

"No."

"All right. I want you to move forward to where you're twenty-five unless something of importance has happened. One . . . two . . . three. What are you doing now? Are you still with the same family?"

"Yes."

"Have you ever gone back to that beautiful place?"

"No, but it haunts me."

"You still there doing the mending and working around the house?"

"Yes, but I also take care of some children."

"Have you ever had a boyfriend or made love with anybody or is it just work?"

"I stay by myself. And I don't like taking care of the children."

"On the count of three, let's move forward to where

you're thirty. One . . . two . . . three. Where are you now?"

"I'm taking the boy to the spring."

"Let's move forward then, on the count of three, to where you're at the spring. One . . . two . . . three."

"I'm just a little far. I want him to go and see what happens if he goes. Now I can see him going. He's sitting on the rock by the water under the tree. He's sitting where I sat. Exactly where I sat."

"And what is happening?"

"He's looking around to see if I'm there. I'm trying to hide."

"Mm-hmh."

"Then I realize I shouldn't hide from him. I just don't want to get too close."

"Let's move forward in time 'til something has happened. One . . . two . . . three. What is happening?"

"Funny, this place. It pulls."

"It what?"

"It pulls."

I was standing some distance away and trying to see what, if anything, was going on. I was curious so my attention was focused in the direction of the spring but it also seemed as if there were something emanating from the place that swept around me and pulled me towards it.

"On the count of three, you will know the mystery of what goes on there and be able to tell me. One . . . two . . . three. What is the mystery of this place? What is the power?"

"The boy's sitting there on the rock and he's looking

at me like he doesn't understand why we've come there. He wants to leave. He's saying, 'Why have we come here? Why are you bringing me here?' Then I say, 'I wanted you to see the water and the trees.' And he says, 'There's no one' and 'Where's the water?' He doesn't even see it! He doesn't see the water!"

"Have him put his feet in it."

"He's frightened. He's frightened of me though. He says I'm talking crazy."

"All right. Are you going to leave there now?"

"He's running back. I'm following and trying to catch him and I'm telling him not to tell anybody I've brought him there."

"All right. On the count of three, you'll be back with the family. One . . . two . . . three. What's happening?"

"His father's very angry with me. He says that I took the boy somewhere, that I shouldn't have taken him without telling people. The boy was very frightened that I was saying strange things. I shouldn't frighten him like that. He's very angry at me and now I know I've lost him completely. I thought maybe if I took care of his children he might like me but he's too frightened of me and now I've frightened his son."

"Is that the same one that you liked before?"

"Yes."

"All right. Let's move forward to where you're thirty-five without any stress or strain. One . . . two . . . three. Are you still there with the same family?"

"No."

"Where are you now?"

"I'm listening to this man."

"What's his name?"

"Peter."

"Ah! Is he known as the apostle?"

"He's known as Peter and the people listen to him but there's a lot of controversy about him."

"Do you like what he says?"

"Yes."

"Does he say the same things your mother was saying?"

"I can't tell. Not really. I don't know if my mother has heard him talk. I haven't seen my mother for a long time."

"On the count of three, I want you to move forward to where you're forty without any stress or strain. One . . . two . . . three. Where are you now?"

"I found my father."

"Your real father?"

"No."

"The one with the bad foot?"

"It's not that bad."

"Oh, is it cured?"

"Yes."

"Who cured it?"

"He said a man cured it."

"Was the man's name Jesus?"

"Yes."

"Mm-hmh!"

"He said all he did was put his hand on it."

"I see. Have you met Jesus?"

"No."

"Are you going to live with your father now?"

"No."

"Does he still live with your mother?"

"I didn't ask. I don't want to know."

"All right."

"I have a feeling something bad has happened to her . . . from him."

"Let's go back with him and ask him so that you know. On the count of three, you will know what has happened to your mother. One . . . two . . . three. What is it?"

"I don't know. He wouldn't say. I think he was embarrassed."

"I see. Let's move forward until you're fifty years of age. One . . . two . . . three. Where are you?"

"I'm not fifty."

"What are you?"

"Forty-seven."

"Are you ill or what is happening?"

"I've come back to the water."

"I see. Let's get the answer then of what the water means. On the count of three, you will know and tell me. One . . . two . . . three. What is the significance of that place?"

"I don't want to leave from here."

"Why?"

"Because it feels real and it's cool and nice."

"Let's move forward in time then to see if you ever leave there, on the count of three. One . . . two . . . three.

Are you still there? Have you died?"

"Yes."

"On the count of three, I want you to go back to where you are forty-seven years of age. You will not have died but it will be the last day of your life in the life we are examining. You will feel no pain or emotion but experience the sensation objectively as an observer. One . . . two . . . three. Where are you now?"

"I'm by the water and I'm thirsty but I don't want to drink."

"Have you ever learned the secret of the water?"

"I'm afraid of it."

"Why are you afraid of it?"

"I don't understand it."

"Is there anybody else there with you?"

"No."

"All right. On the count of three, I want you to leave your physical body and find yourself in spirit just a few moments after experiencing physical death in this incarnation we're now examining. One . . . two . . . three. Where are you now? Again looking down on your body?"

"Yes."

"Okay."

The recorder stopped and Tom brought me out of the hypnotic state. Before the end of this session, I had already pulled back from the past life and my present mind had come to the fore, busy with making meaning of the session.

What was most significant was the perpetual search for spiritual truth, although I doubt I would have phrased the issue just so in that lifetime. This quest colored the entire life or, at least, this version of that life. It was not an academic or even very intentional search for truth. It was an emotionally driven desire to make sense of the conflicting views around me.

In this present lifetime too, I might not have phrased it as a search for spiritual truth. Even before doing the past-life explorations, I was interested in spiritual beliefs. As a girl, it took the form of investigating different religions. When my friends and I had sleepover parties, the topic of conversation, even more than about boys, was religion. Much later I studied formally in theological school. Eventually my searching went beyond traditional practices to a broader and lifelong spiritual quest.

My mother, in the past life, believed in an old form of nature worship that was something of a secret because it was no longer followed by the majority of the people in that area. It is quite possible that she came from some other place where her beliefs had been shared by others. That she persisted in her beliefs against such censure in her adopted society at large and in spite of such ridicule at home certainly demonstrates admirable strength of conviction. The predominant religion in Jerusalem then was Judaism, which was in the process of being challenged by the new Christianity. There were also old and new influences from other religions of the Egyptians, Greeks, and Romans who were making their presence very strongly felt. But for some unknown reason, I felt that the source of my mother's beliefs lay somewhere quite east of the city of Jerusalem. The dynamics of my family in that life were not such that my own learning was helped.

My mother in that life would have liked me to follow in her beliefs but she was reluctant to force the issue because of pressure from her husband, my stepfather. He considered her beliefs and practices complete nonsense and yet he did not seem to follow any other religion very conscientiously. He was probably a Jew as most people were but certainly not a very orthodox one. He would disappear to celebrate some of the holy days elsewhere and would occasionally try to follow some practices at home although doing so was fraught with obstacles from my mother. There were endless arguments between my mother and my stepfather over the issue of religion.

These heated arguments would ignite whenever either one of them tried to carry out some practice of their separate systems or whenever either one of them said anything to us children that might be construed as religious instruction. My mother was firm in her beliefs and could manage to follow them quite nicely on her own. She would have liked her children—myself and his children too—to have followed her ways, but this was too often where the disputes began.

My stepfather was adamant that his children not be handicapped in the world by adhering to what he considered an outmoded religion. When he couldn't win an argument on a strictly theological principle, he inevitably resorted to this argument based on social considerations.

But it was more in reaction to my mother than as

a result of any deep inner conviction of his own that he professed to believe as he did. It was as if the degree of his faith were to be measured by how vehemently he could defend it against all lesser creeds, particularly my mother's.

His personality tended to meanness, which seemed related to his disability. He was not always mean. He was sometimes jovial and a pleasure to be around. However, his good nature seemed to float precariously on a hot sea of anger that could well up unexpectedly at any time into a scalding storm. I think my mother and I both believed that if he could be healed of his crooked foot, his temperament might improve as well. In addition, my mother believed that if she had a hand in healing it, he would come around to an acceptance of her beliefs. Unfortunately for that hope, her attempts at healing depended on his cooperation, which could not be counted on. He would have liked his foot healed but then that would prove her right. Also, he would then be bereft of that one thing his self-identity rested on. He was probably just not willing to give up the familiarity of his infirmity and the excuses it provided for him—for his anger, for not working.

I saw a connection here between my past-life stepfather and my present-life mother. My past-life stepfather had to contend with his disability. My present-life mother gave birth to a son with a disability and after his birth never stopped her efforts to help him and open opportunities for him whenever and wherever she could. Disability factored strongly in both lives.

As for me, my attempts to make sense of the conflicting belief systems in that lifetime constituted a private soul searching. There was no way I could air my thoughts to my mother or to my stepfather without setting off an altercation. It was too highly charged a topic for fruitful discussion. And as I had no help from any other quarter, I was left to my own resources to sort it out.

I had a faint glimmering of a belief that there was a common ground where these disparate beliefs met. But to voice such an idea would probably have been considered blasphemy. I was pulled between these two major persuasions not by the soundness of theological argument but rather by the emotional force of my personal connections with each system. I grew up in my mother's world and took that as the standard by which to measure everything else. Slowly, I came to realize that my mother, in that life, was in the minority, and her beliefs were not at all the standard. I wonder what would have happened had some wise old person seen my struggle and taken me under his or her wing to guide me in my search. As it was, I made very little progress on my own.

The carryover to this life was obvious to me. I have not been content with routine acceptance of creeds or the surface appearance of things but have always wished to know of the spirit that permeates the physical world and the meaning behind the obvious. There are many approaches to metaphysical understanding, all valid and as interesting to me now as they were then.

I share this probing nature with my mother in

this lifetime who appeared to be my stepfather in the Jerusalem lifetime. Her views and mine still do not coincide. She doubts that we could have lived past lives that bear on our present lives but we have been more successful during this lifetime in developing a respect for each other's beliefs. This respect is not merely a matter of "live and let live" but involves taking an active interest in each other's views. She has been interested and supportive of my own explorations in this area as long as they are not harmful to me.

If one does accept reincarnation as a given, then the miracle of being healed by Jesus as mentioned in this past life might well be one reason for one to follow the precepts and practices of Christianity in the present life. The case for such a predisposition cannot be proven. Perhaps it doesn't matter whether or not it is proven. Perhaps the most important issue is that having different beliefs, whether in past or present lives, we manage to respect the differences and learn to find where they meet. In that lifetime, my search for the truth was for one ultimate truth. I didn't see that there could be many versions.

There was also the issue of healing and its connection to the mind. My mother in that lifetime had powers to heal but she recognized that the success of the healing depended on the person's cooperation. Holistic medicine certainly recognizes the power of the mind and emotions in physical healing but, rather than something new, it is just a rediscovery of what has been known before.

This past-life session offered several avenues for further study. For one, I was curious about nature worship—what it was, where it came from, and what role it played in the religious life of the time. It was certainly as appealing to me, as is the Taoist homage to nature, and led me to wonder whether these two threads arose independently or were historically interwoven. I had never before come across in my limited exposure to early Christianity much information about nature worship at the time. Now I began to investigate the matter, but too casually for much success. I realized that aside from genuine interest in the subject, I was also seeking verification of the past life. And as much as I wanted to confirm details from any of the sessions, I also felt I should just let the issue of verification rest for the time being, as Fortune had suggested. So I dropped the research.

I began to wonder, though, how much other history, like nature religions, may be similarly submerged and lost to us today so that only the most conspicuous islands in the sea of human experience are known to us now. If that is the case, what a storehouse of knowledge there is in past-life work! Aside from enriching our general knowledge, we might even find alternative approaches to the problems that have been with us off and on throughout human history and still perplex us today.

Chapter Thirteen
As a Priestess-in-Training in Atlantis

I was now able to sit and do the dialogue with Fortune very well. I would type a question, wait for a response, and then type the response as it came in. I still had trouble believing that I was indeed channeling messages from a spirit guide. Sometimes it would seem quite plausible, but at other times I thought I was deluding myself. Much of the dialogue with Fortune revolved around this issue of trust or, rather, my lack of trust.

For one thing, I had no experience like this before and I didn't know anyone else who had experienced it either, at least not in the form of a dialogue at a keyboard. I had decided to keep what I was doing to myself for the time being. I had too many doubts and too little confidence to risk censure from other people. I felt that eventually I would have some sign or confirmation of its being genuine enough so as to feel comfortable talking about it. But keeping it all to myself meant that, in addition to avoiding possible censure from others, I was also depriving myself of potential support and the possibility of learning of others doing similar work. Of course, Tom knew what I was doing and followed my progress encouragingly, but very few others knew what I was up to. Fortune kept insisting that instead of looking outside myself for approval, I needed to build up an inner trust.

I considered confiding in my mother about this new dialogue writing with Fortune, especially after the past-life session in Jerusalem. I asked Fortune about it. He said it would be good to do eventually but not quite yet. He still insisted on my working through the process by myself as much as possible until it was familiar, easy, and automatic for me. I followed his advice. It was good advice. Too easily influenced by the opinions of others, I might well have abandoned the project altogether had someone, especially my mother, tried to convince me I was mistaken about the endeavor. I wouldn't have had much of anything tangible to justify my efforts in the face of such an argument. Nevertheless, in spite of my own doubts, something kept me at it.

Fortune said I needed to write more. I could write anything I liked and, if I put questions to him, he would respond. Sometimes he would volunteer to teach me something about a subject I hadn't asked about. But still he insisted that it was too soon to look back over what I had written.

Meanwhile, I did another hypnosis session. Tom began as usual.

"On the count of three, I want you to let go of everything and meet your very best friend, Fortune. One . . . two . . . three. How is he doing?"

"He's there and he's very stern-looking. He says he's not going to sit and make any jokes."

"All right. What is the major message he has for you today?"

"He says I'm concerned about a past-life relationship

with someone in my present life. He says I know who he's referring to. He's going to ease the way to go to the past life that has the most to say about what the obstacle is for the current life."

"All right. On the count of three, you will let go of everything and without any stress or strain go back to the lifetime that Fortune is discussing. One . . . two . . . three. You are now fifteen years of age. Where are you? Are you indoors or out-of-doors?"

"Fortune is still there."

"But are you back in this previous lifetime?"

"No. He wants to say first that it will be tricky to work through this one but to stay with it and push into every part of it as much as possible. Go thoroughly and conscientiously and make sure nothing is rushed and everything is absorbed. He says to go gradually into it through the tunnel. It won't be easy to get into it, but carry on."

Once before, Fortune had advised Tom to use the time tunnel to take me into a past life. This time he was giving further instructions. Perhaps Fortune knew exactly what was coming and therefore was guiding these sessions more actively than I had given him credit for. Rather than a haphazard dipping into some bucket of memories, the choice of what I was to re-experience now appeared to be a very deliberate one. Also Fortune seemed to know not only the content of the past life I was about to re-live but also that it would be tricky to get into it and work through it. I wondered what he meant by "tricky."

I did know the person in my present life Fortune referred to. I had mentioned to Tom that I would like to investigate a past-life connection with this person but I gave Tom no details, not even a name. But Fortune knew what I was asking for. It was as if he read my mind and okayed my request for insight into the present relationship. The person in question was a man I was personally involved with. When we first met, there seemed to be an immediate and mutual recognition and attraction. There was however also a strange guardedness, a faint feeling of caution that I could not have explained.

"All right. Ask him if he will stay with us and help me and give me suggestions so that I will know the proper questions to ask and how long to keep you in each area."

"Of course."

Tom proceeded to guide me into his regular tunnel routine but much more gradually than he usually did. As I listened to his instructions and the lengthy description of the tunnel, I was reminded of a tunnel experience I had had years before when I almost died, or maybe did die for a short time, of a severe case of malaria when I was living in Africa. At that time, the tunnel felt like a closing-in, a darkening constriction accompanied by a frightful panic, which then suddenly broke open to glorious light and a vision of such ecstasy that defied description. But the two tunnels had some similarities and my mind jumped back and forth comparing them. Eventually I focused my attention again on the instructions Tom was giving me about the tunnel to a past life.

"You can see the end of the tunnel coming and the light. And now allow it to happen. On the next count you will see or feel or sense yourself in this previous lifetime that Fortune has chosen for us to re-visit at this time. Number one: You are now there. You are now fifteen years of age. I want you to look around and perceive yourself and tell me: Are you indoors or out-of-doors?"

"Outdoors."

"Are you male or female?"

"Female."

"What is your name?"

"I can't tell my name."

"On the count of three, you will know your name."

"I know my name; I can't tell it now."

"Why?"

"Because my name is powerful."

"All right. Are you in a city or in the country?"

"In a city. There are very broad white steps and I'm moving down the steps."

"What country do you live in and what year is it . . . based on our present calendar?"

"We'll come to that later."

My present mind wondered if this reluctance to give information was what Fortune meant by a "tricky" session. I also noticed that my tone of voice sounded remarkably self-assured for a young girl.

"All right. You're moving down the steps and you're fifteen years of age. Do you live in this house where the steps are or what are you doing there?"

"The house with the steps is a temple."

"Have you been worshipping at the temple?"

"I've been with the other students."

"What are you studying for?"

"We're studying the future. We're studying what to do about the future. We're studying our part in it. I've been given a big role."

"Is this a lifetime on the planet we know as Earth?"

"Yes. Very . . . long . . . ago."

"Was this during the time of Atlantis or Lemuria?"

"Yes. Atlantis."

"Mm-hmh! How long have you been in school?"

"For some years. From a small child."

"Do you live with your family at all?"

"No."

"Do you remember your family at all?"

"My family isn't important. I was very young when they knew that I should be one of the students. I left my family. I haven't seen them. I miss them but there's something bigger than that."

"All right. How much longer will you stay in the school?"

"It isn't clear. There's a lot to learn."

"Is there anything you'd like to tell me about your feelings or what you're studying so that we can develop an appreciation of your early life there?"

"I'm frightened because we are learning that this will all end in the future. And I don't want it to end. I want it to continue."

"You mean it will end in your lifetime?"

"I don't know that yet. Our training is to build

ourselves up so that we have the strength and the spirit to make the decisions when the time comes."

"At this time in Atlantis were males and females on an equal level?"

"Oh yes. There are both male and female students."

"Will you become known as priests or part of the work in the temple or will you be out with the other population?"

"It depends on how quickly we learn. Each step is very important. Not everybody that begins ends it as well. It's very important to do each step because there is so much and it all is built on what came before. If you don't complete one thoroughly, when you come to the next one it all falls apart and sometimes you can't continue. You fall apart yourself."

The emphasis on sequence and order in learning reminded me of the Montessori method of education. I had trained and worked as a Montessori teacher. The sequencing and ordering of learning tasks made sense to me, unlike some others who found those aspects of the Montessori method unnecessary and restrictive. But I was too involved in the past life to dwell on the comparison for long.

"So from a child, I began the training and I'm learning but it's very hard learning and you can't know everything at one time. You have to trust that a little bit comes and then a little bit more and this is very important."

"Just so that I can picture you better, would you describe yourself to me?"

"I'm tall."

"How tall . . . based on our present measurements?"

"Like a tall man, but I'm a woman."

"Six—?"

"And I'm very beautiful and the beauty comes from being the chosen."

I interrupted Tom here. I didn't like his emphasis on mere physical looks and then to bring an already unimportant topic down to measuring it with numbers was even more tedious.

"Are you blond, brunette? What color are your eyes?"

"I have dark hair but it is changing color."

"What is it becoming?"

"I don't know, but it will change."

"Are your eyes blue or brown?"

"They're blue and they see far. They're strange eyes, I know."

"When you take your training, is it all lectures, or do you study books? Do you have physical exercise? Do you live in a school or the temple?"

"We do all those things. We listen. We tune the senses. We do very fine tuning of the senses. When you're little, you learn the senses very roughly and when you get older, you tune them higher and higher so that the vibrations between the differences become very fine and I'm very good at that."

"Will you remember how to do that so that in your present incarnation you will be able to do it at least to some degree to help people?"

"This takes a lot of training. You can't just want it to be."

"Can you transfer that training from your lifetime in Atlantis to your present incarnation?"

"I've done some already. I know so much of it already but there are obstacles. There are always obstacles."

"I see."

"Different colors appear very strong when they are next to each other but you can take a color and see different shades of it very close. Then you get trained to see finer and finer gradations of color . . . finer and finer . . . until you can see more than the color."

I was describing gradations of hue but the work included gradations of shade as well. In the beginning exercises for small children, the difference between any two colors placed side by side was great—"strong when next to each other"—and therefore easy to distinguish. Gradually the difference between two adjoining colors was lessened so that the perception was trained to finer and finer attunement. I was familiar with this exercise as part of the Montessori early childhood teaching.

However, in Atlantis the exercise went further. In the midst of a person's attempt to distinguish between two very similar colors, the mind would often rebel, escaping from the exercise at hand to a greater "vision." The exercises had this double purpose—to train visual perception and also to constrict the attention progressively to a breaking point so that one might explode into sudden enlightenment, although this latter occurrence—"seeing more than the color"—was rare.

"And the same thing with the taste and with the sound and with the touching. You start with the very big coarse differences and you develop a very fine sense. The training of the children is like that. It's an important part of the training, but it's not all of the training."

I was struck again by the similarity between these methods and those that constitute the sensorial component of the Montessori Method of early education that I had been trained in and taught in my present life. But again, I was too absorbed in the past life to linger over these thoughts.

"As we go along in this lifetime, will you keep in mind that we will overcome all of the obstacles as they occur so that you will be able to transfer this magnificent training to your present incarnation and it will help you in fulfilling your role on Earth in your present incarnation in helping the world to learn to live a better life, a life totally and completely filled with love? Will you commit to do that?"

I was annoyed by this question. Yes, the connection to the Montessori training was there, but I felt that what I was revealing was being pulled to some other purpose, to fit some notion of Tom's. I didn't think Tom understood that the obstacles were to be respected and could not just be willed away.

"This information is very tricky. It depends on so many things. You see we're studying the future but there are very big cycles. We're coming to the end of a big one and a new one will start very fresh. And there will always be at the end of a cycle the people that will carry the information to the next cycle but it has to be built up in each cycle by the souls that are in that cycle so that it is re-learned and re-learned because there is always the other side that is the test to keep the cycle going."

"How many years does a cycle take?"

"We're at 13,000 now, and they haven't told us when it's going to end."

Tom seemed interested more in establishing dates than in investigating the idea of cycles. I was wishing he would ask about "the other side that is a test" because his questions usually evoked more elaboration. Nevertheless, I had a vague idea of what was involved which was that each cycle had its own lessons to be learned and that along with the learning there were tests or challenges to the learning. The people in any cycle had to keep passing the tests as they appeared or the whole cycle was threatened.

"Can you project yourself forward to your present incarnation and tell us where we are in a cycle at the present time?"

"It isn't a question of where the time is. The crucial question is whether the people are aware that a cycle can end. I can't tell in years but there's a big lesson . . . a big lesson."

"I realize that. I'm only asking questions from my limited knowledge but I think there are people alive now who have been in similar training to yours in the same or other cycles. I am concerned that you too bring forward this knowledge into your present incarnation so that we may have the advantage of that knowledge to help our present civilization."

"I can't answer that now."

"All right. Is there anything else you'd like to tell me or shall we move forward to the end of your next breakpoint or section in your training?"

"We are just completing a small part."

"All right. On the count of three, move forward until you're almost at the end of the next phase so that you can tell me what you have learned and the knowledge you have gained. One . . . two . . . three. Where are you now, what is your age and what are you doing? Are you still studying at the temple?"

"I'm having a hard time. There's another student that I like very much. He's also been in training from when he was very young. The training is very strict. I see him and I talk to him but I can't talk to him very much."

"What is his name?"

"I don't know his name."

"Why don't you ask him what his name is when you have a chance to talk to him?"

"Names are very special. You can't just ask somebody their name like that."

"Can you tell me what your name is?"

"No."

"Can you tell me how old you are now?"

"I'm sixteen."

"How are you doing in your studying?"

"It's becoming a problem because I'm being very distracted by this student."

"Are you having physical desires and wanting to spend time with this student?"

"Yes. I think he feels the same way."

"Is this forbidden?"

"Yes."

"Do you, in your present incarnation, know this student?"

"Yes."

"Do you know what this person's name is?"

"I can't tell the name."

"I mean his name in your present incarnation."

"I know. I know who it is."

"Well, will you tell me, please?"

"I can't tell the name."

"Why?"

"It's something about telling names."

"Well, in your present incarnation, telling names does not have any real significance as it did back then in your training."

Oh, yes, it most certainly does, I thought, *but maybe not in exactly the same way.* Names had intrinsic power then and were used like totems for one's personal identity. The choice of a name was a serious business and left to those who knew about such things. Names were not used casually as they are now to call a person to you or to identify someone.

"But I would like to get the name on record so we have the knowledge of who this person is in your present incarnation."

"I can't say it now. Maybe I can say it later."

Much, much later, I thought to myself. By now all the questions about the name had pulled me out of the past life and into the present. With Tom's next question though, I sank back into the past life again.

"All right. What have you learned? What new knowledge have you gained?"

"I am having trouble. The lessons tell us that the training is dependent on the whole group doing the training. Everybody in the training is doing it together and every piece of that group is important. Everybody must be totally in it. If somebody changes the vibration either willfully or involuntarily, it brings the level of the whole group down. It's the same with the whole civilization. And I'm afraid I'm bringing it down because I can't concentrate. I keep thinking about this person and I'm bringing the level down and I don't want to do that."

"All right. On the count of three, you will be able to eliminate this person from your thoughts. One . . . two . . . three. How are you doing now?"

"I can't eliminate him from my thoughts. I'm going to see the woman, the old woman that knows about the training. She was the one that decided when I was very young that I should do the training. She's like a living angel. And she will know what I should do."

"All right. On the count of three, you will be with her and describe what happens. One . . . two . . . three.

"She's so full of light. It's wonderful just to be with her. She says it is very difficult. She says this is one of the greatest difficulties—to be able to see a larger important role for oneself and be able to reconcile it with one's personal life and desires. She says this is always an issue and she knows it's hard for me. She knew that it was going to happen because it had been predicted but she didn't want to say anything to me before to make it happen. She knows the person, without my saying, that I am attracted to. She said that we are both very high souls and it is because of that we can recognize each other. It will always be a question of how much we can recognize and be with each other and still do the work that we know is important. She says that she knows what the outcome will be but she can't tell me. She says that I have to work at it, figure it out for myself. I have to choose whether I leave the training or whether I continue the training and how I am to do it. She said that it's very wise of me to come to her and that I will be taking on a lot of what she is because in many, many lifetimes to come there will be people that come to see me as I am coming to see her, not so much for words, but just for being in my presence and if I choose well, I can allow something greater to come through that will be of help. Then she says she doesn't want to talk about this now because I can't . . . I won't hear it from her. I won't be able to focus on it because I'm only interested in this young man. She says to think about it and come back again. It will demand much work in the thinking but I should do it. So I'm going away."

"All right. On the count of three, you make a decision and you're ready to go back and talk to her. One . . . two . . . three. You have been doing a lot of thinking. What have you been thinking about and what is your decision? Are you going to go back and see the woman?"

"I'm going back to see her again. I've thought about it and I'm asking her. I said I can't make a choice because

I don't know what is the future of any of the choices—if I leave the training, if he leaves the training (and I'm not even sure that he would because I can't really talk to him about it) or if we both leave the training just to be with each other. I don't know what will happen. It's not a clear future. So I can't choose because I don't know what the future is."

"You don't know what choices you have."

"She says, okay, it's clear that I've thought about it but not knowing the future is not a sufficient excuse. She says that I've gone far enough in the training to know that you don't have to know the future to make a choice, that you make it for the moment you're in from going inside to the heart and knowing that that is the right thing to do. She says that she knows it's not proper in the training to have certain conversations. But she suggests that I send my thoughts to this person and ask if he has anything to say about it. So I'm going to do that. She says not to do it when the others are around, to do it when I'm by myself. I'm not by myself but she says it doesn't take long and that I know that. It's a question of the attitude and the mental vibration. She says I know the name of the state of mind, the exercise to get into it and, when I get into it, that it's momentary. I can shoot the thought and aim well. He'll know and he will send it back."

"All right. On the count of three, you will have done this and received your answer. One . . . two . . . three. What did you receive? First of all, what did you send him?"

"I sent that I have to make a choice and that it

involves him and the training and I don't know what to do and I wonder what he thinks."

"What did he answer you?"

"He says, yes, he knows. He was waiting for me to say something. He says he's trying with the same decision. He says it's very difficult, he doesn't know what to do but that we should at least agree that if either of us knows what to do we should tell the other one. But I don't know about that because I'm afraid of making a decision based on his. I think I should it do it without that."

"Based solely upon your own desires and needs."

I knew the issue for me just then wasn't a matter of trying to satisfy personal desires and needs but rather whether I should go "inside to the heart" to make a decision myself or turn to the young man for help in making the decision. And of course the decision would affect others.

"The old woman said I should make a decision myself. It's so hard to do the training with this."

"I can understand that. But you are a very self-disciplined person, aren't you?"

I wasn't sure if Tom was being sarcastic or hopeful with this statement because it didn't seem to me that I had much self-discipline at all.

"I'm going back to see the woman again. She says I should leave the training, not forever, but she says I'm too agitated now. I should go take my physical body and move it far enough that my senses are not dealing with the training and they're not dealing with him. I should allow only my mind to visit the training and him without my physical body there."

Removing the physical body from "the scene of the crime" and depriving the senses of their source of stimulation seemed to rest on a certain assumption about the mind. The assumption is that the mind is made of finer stuff, is more capable of understanding the larger picture yet needs sometimes to be kept from the corrupting influence of the coarser and wayward world of the physical senses. The physical senses have an immediate and necessary but myopic viewpoint. Perhaps this was about "getting away from it all."

"She is giving me some exercises to do. She says I haven't learned them yet in the training but that I will need them for this decision-making. So I'm leaving her and going away."

"You're not even going back to the school at all?"

"I'm going to do a retreat."

"All right. On the count of three, you will be wherever you go for your retreat. One . . . two . . . three. Where are you now?"

"It's a very small little building. It's amongst some trees and very near some water. It's on a very, very steep hill and I'm sitting in it. It's open all around. It's like a pedestal with columns and it's very beautiful. I would just like to stay here and not make any decision at all and I know that's not right. But for right now, I'm just going to enjoy this beautiful place. I haven't started to do the exercise she told me. But she told me to come here."

"Are you a long ways from the school, your training center?"

"It's not so far in reality, but it's far enough."

The building was a gazebo. It looked like something out of a Maxfield Parrish painting. The setting, on a wooded hillside overlooking the water, was very romantic. The structure itself was made of a round platform with round columns around the circumference of the platform. At the back, the platform was level with the hillside and joined it with a small step. The slope of the hill was such that the front side was very far from the ground and supported underneath like a pedestal. The local people revered this special place where people came to sit and think looking out to the water in hopes of pulling themselves to a decision. Offerings of fruit and nuts were made to whoever was in residence. Physically, it was not at all far from the temple but it didn't need to be as the place itself claimed a certain isolation from everything, even from the people who came close enough to offer food.

"All right. Let's move forward to where you have been there for a while. One . . . two . . . three. You have now been there for some time. What is happening and what have you done?"

"I've done her exercise. I've done the mental one. I can pull in the view of the training and I'm seeing what they're doing but it's not very clear because I'm not very good at it. It's hard to do. It takes a lot of energy and I get tired. But there are people here that bring fruit and they always honor people that are coming here to make decisions like this. So I'm thanking them and I'm doing my physical exercises for the body to get clear."

"Were the exercises the old woman gave you both mental and physical?"

"She gave me the mental one but I know that I need to do the physical one, too. I'm doing it."

"All right. Let's move forward a little bit farther. One . . . two . . . three. You're at a decision point. What are you doing?"

"I can't do it."

"What can't you do?"

"I can't do the decision. The whole thing seems to be pulling me apart. I'm forgetting the training. I can't see him there. I can't see him when I do the mental exercise. He isn't there."

"Has he left the school also?"

"I don't know for sure. I'm thinking he must be doing the same thing. I don't see him when I look at the school."

"What do you do? Do you go back to see the old woman?"

"I'm leaving the pedestal."

This was highly unorthodox. The whole point of the place was to be a retreat where one could ponder a difficult decision. One showed respect for its purpose by going there only when necessary and staying only as long as one needed to make whatever decision was sought. But one didn't leave the pedestal until arriving at a clear and firm resolution. My being there in the first place was the result of preferential treatment and now I was abusing the privilege by not staying through until a decision had been made.

"I'm very shaken. I can't eat the fruit they bring . . . and . . ." I sighed, "Oh!"

"What is happening?"

"I'm very weak. I tripped coming from the pedestal and I've fallen down the stairs that go to the water."

"Are you in the water now?"

"No, just near it. They're picking me up. They're taking me somewhere to take care of me."

"Have you lost a lot of weight?"

"No. It's just that my parts are coming apart. I can't pull together the physical and the mental and the spiritual. It's all going in different directions and I think I'm going crazy. They've sent a message to the old woman. They know that she sent me here."

"Can you tell me the name of the young man in the school now, his name in your present incarnation?"

"No. And the old woman is coming."

"What does she tell you and what is happening?"

"She says that she gave me a task that she thought I could do. But there are others that disagree with her about my being ready to do it. She says that it will be very difficult now for me to try to pull everything together enough to come back to the training. She says she wants very much for me to try to do that because she's also involved in it now for having pushed me past where I've had the training. She says that I need to pull myself together first and to forget about the decision for now— just pull myself together and get myself back to the training. She's saying a lot of things. I don't understand the words."

"Say the words."

"She's doing some prayers. I don't understand them."

"Can you repeat them?"

"Oh, no! I couldn't do that."

"Why?"

"They're special prayers. I can't say all the words. She can say them. She knows them and she's trained to do them. If I do that, it would only be worse. I can't say them."

"Will you remember them so that when we have brought you out of this, you will be able to—"

"I can't say them! If you don't have the training, you can't say them. I can hear them but I can't repeat them."

"I see. What do you do now? Do you go back to the school—the training center?"

"She's gone and she sends me messages. I'm trying to pull myself together. This has become a very big issue at the school. It has disrupted things further. I can talk about it now from another place but I can't talk about it from in the body because it's too broken."

"All right. Talk about it from wherever you can so that we can relive it and record it."

"I'm not in the body but I'm attached to it still. They're taking care of the body. It isn't healing. It wasn't such a severe fall but it isn't healing. They're doing all these things and trying to make it heal. The old woman has come again and she says I will only get better when I decide myself to pull all the parts together. She said I can't avoid things. I have to come and bring the spirit back to the body. She's talking to me over my body. I can see her doing that. I can hear her. I know her care and concern. But I can't go back into the body because then I still have to make the decision. She says, "Yes, but you have to do that. If you don't do it now, you'll have to do it later.' She says, 'Just bring it all back together. No one will ask you to make a decision. You can go to the training and continue. You can leave the training. You can go with him. But don't think of the decision itself as so big. You'll do what's right.' She's telling me these things to comfort me but I can't pull it all together."

"All right, let's move forward just a little bit in time to see what happens. One . . . two . . . three. Where are you now?"

"Now I'm seeing how I'm selfish, how I need just to pull myself together, if not for me or anybody then because it's pulling down the whole training, pulling down the others. They can't concentrate. The vibration has changed. And I realize that I've been responsible for that. And I need to come back into the body so I'm doing that now. I'm going to make myself heal."

I was crying.

"And I'm so sorry." I sighed.

"It's all right. Without any emotional stress now of any kind, no trauma. You have now healed yourself and are now well, aren't you?"

"There are scars but I can manage for now."

"Physical scars or mental scars?"

"Deeper scars."

"All right. Do you go back to the school?"

"Yes."

"All right. How is it going at school now?"

"They're doing an exercise for my return. I must go to each person." I was crying again. "I must ask for forgiveness from each person . . . and they must forgive me before I can go the next person in the circle. I'm so sorry they have to do that. I know I've been disruptive. I didn't mean to be."

"I think they know that, don't they?"

"They say it will be a long time before the level comes up again. But each one is forgiving me." I sighed very deeply.

"Is the young man there too?"

"I haven't come to him yet. They're each forgiving me as I'm going around the circle and they're saying that it's a good lesson. I see him there. I don't know if I can ask his forgiveness. I'm coming to where he is. He's standing there and I can't understand. He's acting like this has nothing to do with him. He's standing just like the others. I come to him and I'm looking at him and I can't believe he can just stand there like the others. I've passed by him. I'm going around the rest of the circle."

"Did he forgive you?"

"Yes, but it was very perfunctory."

"All right. Let's move forward 'til you've gone around the whole circle."

"I have."

"Everybody has forgiven you?"

"Yes."

"Okay. And you realize now that your young man

was not feeling the same things you were, was he?"

"He was, but he kept it to himself. I don't think it's going to work."

"Well, let's move forward a little to see how things are going. Let's move to where you have completed this phase on the count of three. One . . . two . . . three. You still at the school?"

"Yes."

"How are you doing? Much better now?"

"I'm making a lot of effort. But this thing has stayed there. It has affected the training. I can see that it's not exactly the same. I don't know if it's just my perception or whether it's really happening but it's as if people try to avoid me. They don't really avoid me because they've forgiven me. They're carrying on, but there's this little doubt about whether I would do it again. They're just a little bit leery of me. And it's persisting between him and me."

"As strong as before?"

"Yes. More so."

"Does he pay any attention to you?"

"He's denying it. And I'm just going to have to leave the training. I can't have this continue. I can't have it happen again. So I'm going to the old woman and I'm saying this just keeps going on and on. She says yes. She seems to be on the edge of her patience with me. She says, 'You have something that is very strong which is that you want to deal with whatever it is and that is what he's not doing. He's not dealing with it. He's denying it.'"

"And it will harm him more in the long run, won't

it?"

"She's saying that she hopes the training will be enough to help him because it will take so much more energy to keep something like that from acknowledgment. She can't talk to him directly. He has somebody else he can turn to but she knows from the other person that he isn't doing that, that he's become very much unto himself. He's pulled himself away and he does what's the minimum and he's straining himself."

"Mm-hmh."

"She said it's a problem because both of us need to do the training and we both want to do it. We have a greater sense of what the whole group is about. From an early age it's been clear that both of us are to do this work. It's so obvious that we're so in tune. She says before when this kind of thing happened, it was so clear-cut. People leave the training or people just decide to dispense with the personal and they take on another side training just to help them do that. It's an additional bunch of exercises that they do and it helps to control that. She says she doesn't really know what to do at this point or what to advise me. I'm feeling lost because I count on her. She says, no, that's where I'm wrong, that I don't realize how much I'm doing on my own and with all the help of the training and knowledge. She says, 'You're tapping into something greater and that something greater will help you. You don't need me. In fact, you're going to go way beyond me and you're doing it already because you're looking at all of this. That's where your strength is. And that's where the other people fear you because you're developing a strength that's greater than the training but you don't know it. They can develop it too. There's nothing so special about you that they can't do it too. Everybody can do it. He can do it too but he's going to have a problem because he won't acknowledge this crisis in his life.'"

"What decision do you make?"

"I've decided to leave the training. I've decided not to do the rest of training."

"How many more years, approximately, would it take?"

"Oh, this is something that continues to go on. You always carry on with the group. Then you take on your own task. I haven't finished the training but I'm going to have to take on my own task without the training because I can't stay there. I feel better making the decision."

"Okay. Then let's move forward on the count of three until you have taken on your own task. One . . . two . . . three. Where are you now and what are you doing?"

"I'm going down to the same place where I went for the retreat. I go down to the water. I'm going to do something on my own that I'm not sure is going to work. I'm going to take a boat with things to eat so I can survive. I'm going to go out on the water. I'm going to go until I know what to do next. My decision to take on a task has come before its time and I can't have any help now from the other people. I'll have to decide myself without the blessing of the training. So I'm going down. I'm taking the boat. I feel a certain sadness and the greatest sadness is leaving him."

"Anything else, or shall we take you forward to where you're out on the boat?"

"I'm on the boat."

"What is happening? Are you at a decision point? Let's move forward on the count of three. One . . . two . . . three. Would you tell me what is happening, please?"

"I can't see anymore."

"Have you died? Has your spirit left your body?"

"Yes."

"I want you to go back . . ."

"I haven't died."

"Okay. Well, then what is happening? Are you in the boat? Lying down in the boat?"

"I can't see . . . I can't see anymore."

"All right. Would you say you're still alive?"

"I don't think so."

What was happening here was something new. I hadn't died and I wasn't living in the past life either. Rather I just couldn't see anything. It came in from all sides at once, like an old photograph fogging up at the edges until the whole picture was obscured. At first, I thought it was fog on the lake but I couldn't see from myself and I couldn't see to myself. It was as if a gauzy cloth was placed between myself and everything else. I wondered if this was the renowned veil of mystical literature. I had been allowed to see only so much and that was it. I could not penetrate the veil.

"Well, let's go back now, on the count of three, to where you were still alive. One . . . two . . . three. You're now in the boat but you're still alive. How long have you been out in the boat?" Tom paused.

"Hmm?"

I was struggling to pull in the picture but couldn't at all. I tried to piece together from memory what I had just seen trying to hold onto it like a vanishing dream but all in vain. I felt myself coming back to present reality. It was frustrating not to be able to recapture what was so vivid just moments before. Tom kept trying to find out what was happening.

"Please talk to me."

"I'm seeing . . ."

"You're seeing what?"

"Fortune is there."

"Are you still alive now?"

"No."

"All right. Did you die from hunger or thirst or just decide to die or what happened? Please tell me."

"Fortune is there and he says there's more to learn from that, but not now."

"All right. Would you tell me now what the name of the young man in that lifetime is in this lifetime so that you have it recorded?"

"I'm asking Fortune. Fortune says I don't need to tell the name if I don't want to."

"Well, it's up to you."

"He says take a few moments and relax. He says be content not to know everything. He says mysteries will remain."

"I see."

"He says the difficulty is in the process itself. He says

certain things I'm not ready for yet. And he says I can't know everything about that lifetime now."

"Ask him if you have many new powers that are going to be given to you in the future."

"He says the powers are there. It's the obstacles to using them and knowing of them that are the question."

"Ask him if he will work with us in overcoming those obstacles."

"He says this is a major task. This is a serious job and it'll go on for a long time. He says that I've embarked on it, that I'm doing well but that it's not something that can be learned quickly at all. Even the steps in the progress of the whole thing cannot be laid out. He said that I need to respect that one cannot ask and have all the answers at once. When one pushes and wants to go further than one can do, even in that lifetime. If one goes too fast on major work like this, it splinters and disintegrates. One must be very careful. Fortune says it's important that I work at it but that I have to be patient with the process. And he says, of course he will help and there's more help coming than just from him. He says some people work at this in the context of certain groups or traditions. Some people work very solitary. He said that my work is pushed along by certain people and helped greatly by people like you. He says my present connection with this person that I've asked about is very important. He says I know that. And he says the obstacle is there for a purpose."

"Is your relationship with this person going to be a very positive one?"

"He says yes and he says again I'm working on it

and paying attention to it and he is now, too. He also recognizes the importance of it but he doesn't see some aspects of it that I already see and I should be patient with that. He says he's also a bit frightened of the connection but won't admit it. He says things will become clear soon and it's good that I'll be traveling because it will become even clearer. And as much as possible to let it just go on as it is for now."

"All right."

"He says he has one other thing to say about this person. He says there is a feeling that he has more access to the secrets because he has done the training and he can point to it and say, 'I've done the training.' He thinks because he's gone through all this, that he has awareness and the evolution of his spirit in hand. But there is also the separate way which I'm doing which is important and equally valid and can even be more evolved but that doesn't matter. He says the point is not to feel the competition but to go my separate path. To be in relationship, yes, but as far as the work and evolution goes, to trust that I'm doing fine for myself without comparison to others."

"Mm-hmh! All right. Ask him if I may use my prayer that I do at the end of sessions now?"

"He says, 'Sure, anything that will help.'"

Tom said his prayer and proceeded to bring me out of the session. As I emerged from hypnosis, I was preoccupied not with Fortune's concluding advice but with the sudden curtailment of the past-life part of the session. When the veil appeared, I was confused. I didn't understand what was happening. The veil was not part of the past life but rather hung between that past life and my perception of it. As the past life faded, my present mind took over. Despite Tom's suggestions to return to the past life, I couldn't do so. Rather I found myself with Fortune, who explained the difficulty.

The abrupt finish seemed to bother Tom even more than it did me. I was surprised and confused but also content just to see what would happen next. This resignation or acquiescence is typical of the highly suggestible state of hypnosis. One doesn't feel like fighting the system. I was quite willing to "go with the flow." But that acquiescing part of me was also trying to accommodate Tom's instructions to reverse directions and go backwards. Allowing myself to be pulled in these two opposite directions created a tension within me that did not subside until Tom also resigned himself to letting it all take its natural course rather than forcing it into a certain direction.

Fortune's explanation of the veil was that it served to prevent my experiencing what was unnecessary. This made sense, but how it worked intrigued me. Who was it that was deciding what I should see or not see? If these were my own memories, then what mechanism was it that allowed me to remember some and then cut off the rest? It seemed Fortune had a big hand in it but that only made Fortune even more of an enigma. If Fortune was an entity separate from myself, why did he go to such lengths so unselfishly to help me? And how did he know what would and would not be of help? If, instead,

Fortune was my own inner mind and I was in ultimate control, then I must have been pulling the veil over my own eyes.

Another difficulty of this past-life session was that it was hard to describe details of the life in Atlantis. For example, to explain in modern terms the restraints on using names, the details of the various training exercises and my personal disintegration, that is, the falling apart of the physical, mental and spiritual systems was practically impossible. It all rested on a knowledge that we, or at least I, don't possess nowadays.

Perhaps all that knowledge is still intact on the subconscious level. This is what Tom was aiming for when he suggested that I bring forward that knowledge into this lifetime, a suggestion that strangely I kept resisting during the session. Perhaps the reason that more knowledge was not forthcoming was that the personal issues needed sorting out first. There seems to be a sort of gravitational pull towards those personal issues with a high emotional charge. They seem to demand resolution first before one is able to see clearly through to what is neutral information. After all, I was looking for clues to understanding a personal relationship; I hadn't asked to learn about daily life in Atlantis.

The reason I had asked to review this past life in the first place was to help understand a present-life relationship. Seeing the past life was of some help and Fortune's comments helped further. Perhaps more will become clear in time. There certainly was the same unmistakable pull towards each other in both lifetimes. In the present lifetime, I met this man in a spiritual martial arts training that I joined as well. He was dedicated to this endeavor, so dedicated that it took priority over personal relationships. It became obvious after a while, and with the help of this look at a possible past life together, that his priority was clearly in his work. The martial art was not a path that I chose to pursue, much as I respected it. Surely the unresolved conflict of that past life—the choice between a personal relationship versus separate duties to some larger order (the training, the work)— seemed characteristic of our current relationship as well. In our present lives, we were drawn to each other but were fearful, he more than myself, that our friendship might jeopardize our commitments to work which we viewed as larger than ourselves. Our former status as students was a helpful way for me to see us as working on separate but equally important assignments in the classroom of life.

The result was that, in our present lives, he continued with the martial arts training and teaching. while I dropped out of that training. We ended the personal relationship amicably as we both continued on our separate life paths. In spite of the veil that clouded over and ended my glimpse into that past life, I was able to see enough to bring a lesson about that particular past-life relationship into the present life relationship..

The theme of learning lessons in their proper time was also a part of the training at the temple in Atlantis. One step was to be completed before the next step was attempted. I spoke of this early in the session and then myself became a victim of going beyond one's level prematurely. When the old woman sent me on the retreat, I was jumping ahead too fast. I couldn't meet the demands of the retreat and disintegrated as a result. Then again, before reaching the stage at which I was entitled to the "job counseling" the training offered, I set off appointing myself a task. The veil precluded my seeing the results. Perhaps I was spared from witnessing an even worse disaster.

Fortune reiterated the importance of moving along patiently at an appropriate pace with one's learning. Apparently this lesson is one I have needed still to learn in this lifetime. Before I embarked on the past-life work, I was married to a man from Africa and went to live with him there. I remember how often, when I was living in Africa, people there found it fitting to tell me the proverb: "You don't test the depth of the river with both feet." This is a lesson that pops up from time to time, and not surprisingly. We live in a time when our lives, at least in this country, seem to have sped up. We want things now and that desire for immediate gratification carries over into the realm of information and knowledge, spiritual knowledge often included, at least for me. Some things just can't be rushed, including even the learning of that truth.

Fortune brought up another issue from the past-life portion of the session. He said there are many ways of learning. Some will learn through association with groups or traditions. Others will opt for a separate and solitary path. I seem to have chosen the latter both in this lifetime and the past one in Atlantis whereas my "classmate" then chose to stay with the group and now follows a tradition in martial arts with its own group of adherents as well. The past life and Fortune's comments helped remind me that such different approaches need not compete with each other but are all equally valid. It is reassuring to have such a vote of confidence in one's own particular way. It is all the more urgent for anyone living in an advertising age in which persistent and sophisticated persuasion is designed to lead one astray of oneself towards things one doesn't need at all.

Lastly, there was the issue of my indecisiveness, which has carried over into this lifetime too. I have been annoyed at my own inability to make decisions at times, but I had always considered it merely a weakness of character. I didn't see that indecisiveness could also have repercussions beyond oneself. The Atlantis lifetime was an example of how indecisiveness can affect others to such an extent that it can be pure selfishness to indulge oneself in such prolonged vacillation. Any hesitation to act can affect a whole group just as much as any deliberate but inappropriate action.

Indecisiveness also reflects an inability to trust, for there is inherent in any commitment to action the belief in what guides that action. In Atlantis, I hesitated to make the decision about the training on the excuse that I couldn't foresee a guaranteed outcome for either course of action. But one need not know, as the old woman said, the specific outcome before acting. Ultimately, it becomes a matter of trust in that which lies beyond our limited conscious minds, which we misconstrue as the sole decision-makers. Just as the decision of one individual part can affect the group as a whole, so conversely, does the whole—a much greater whole—affect the decision of any part. Making a decision requires trust in the wisdom of that greater whole.

Chapter Fourteen
As Syzzyx in a Future Life

At this point, it seemed these past-life explorations were drawing to a close. It wasn't a matter, as it was before, of being overwhelmed and needing a break to sort things out. Rather the time had come to complete the explorations. I could always continue to carry on conversations with Fortune on my own.

Tom asked what I might like to do in the last session. Occasionally in the past, Tom had asked if I would be interested in looking at a future life. I hadn't liked even thinking about this because my mind would immediately get entangled in all sorts of questions about predestination versus free will. Was everything yet to happen already decided and just waiting for the proper moment to occur? Or were we constantly making the future and throwing it into the past? Or, perhaps, is it all happening at once but on different planes of existence? I had not been eager to delve into these puzzles nor into anything that toyed with my normal sense of time. In addition, as I was feeling the impending conclusion of all these sessions, I didn't want to launch into some entirely new facet of it.

But I had no other agendas at the moment. I had relived a number of past lives. Perhaps it was appropriate to end the whole project with a look at a future life . . . if possible. I knew well enough by now to leave the decision to Fortune.

Tom had done future life sessions with other people before. He said it was difficult for people to describe life that had not become familiar as yet. However, as I had proved to be a good subject so far, he thought it worth a try. So I agreed. Tom hypnotized me, and, as usual, began by consulting Fortune.

"I want you to revisit your wonderful guide and good friend, Fortune, and to do whatever Fortune directs us to do, hopefully a forward life. On the count of three, you will be with Fortune. One . . . two . . . three. How is he doing? Is he on his rock?"

"He's there."

"All right. On the count of three, will you go to the forward lifetime that Fortune wants you to go to? And Fortune, will you go with her? What does he say?"

"He says, 'Yes, do the future life now' and he says to ask for description as detailed as possible when you do it but not any numerical description. No numbers."

"No numbers. Can I ask what year it is?"

"'That's numbers,' he says."

"Okay. On the count of three, you will move forward, without any stress or strain, to that future lifetime. One . . . two . . . three. You are now fifteen years of age. Where are you? Are you indoors or out-of-doors?"

"Outdoors."

"Are you male or female?"

"Female."

"What's your name? On the count of three, you will know. One . . . two . . . three. What is it?"

"Syzzyx."

"Syzzyx. Are you on . . . the planet Earth?"

"Well, yes."

"All right. Do you live with your family?"

"No.

"And how old are you now?"

"Eighteen."

"What do you do?"

"I'm speaking."

"You're speaking?"

"I'm speaking to a group of people."

"I see. What is your subject?"

"History. I'm speaking of learning from past history."

"Mm-hmh! Have there been any bad wars or nuclear wars in the history?"

"There have been some bad wars. The world is all re-arranged."

"Did they use nuclear or more conventional weapons?"

"Everybody's tried everything and the earth itself has warred against itself."

"And the earth itself has what?"

"Warred on itself."

"Mm-hmh! Have most of the people on the earth been killed off?"

"Very, very many."

"Do you have a good civilization now? And a good life?"

"There are two very different groups. There are those that know and those that don't know. Those that don't know are starting fresh. Those that know are trying to teach the ones that don't know."

"I see."

"I'm one of the ones that know."

"Are you lecturing to people that don't know?"

"Yes."

"How do they receive your lecture?"

"It's not clear."

"What is it that you know that they don't know?"

"I know . . . so many things."

"Well, when you make the statement 'those that know' and 'those that don't know,' is that those people who are educated and those that are not? Or what is the difference?"

"The people that don't know are like animals. They're just surviving. They're just trying to live. They're just trying to stay alive."

"I see. Do they live in caves or do they live in buildings? How do they live?"

"They don't even care. They can live anywhere. They're like animals. They're just all over and they're like animals."

"Do they attempt to attack you?"

"Oh, well, they know better than that."

My future mind (which was comparable to my past mind in past-life sessions) was involved in describing that life but my present mind looking in found it all rather humorous. The "ones that don't know" looked like cartoon characters. Their look made sense to me because if indeed this was a future life, I could only imagine it able to be seen in the roughest form.

"Do they outnumber the ones that know? Or which is the larger population?"

"It seems like the ones that don't know," I said exasperatedly, "are very many."

"I'm not permitted to ask you any numbers but is this many, many centuries beyond your present incarnation?"

"It doesn't really matter. There have been so many changes anyway."

"Well, let's concentrate on the people that know. Do you live in houses?"

"We try to."

"Are the houses you live in left over from previous times?"

"A few."

"Don't you build any now?"

"It's just that there's so much fighting so that things are built so quickly and destroyed so quickly."

"What do they use for fighting?"

"Anything."

"That tells me nothing. Do they use swords?"

"They even throw each other around."

"Do they use guns? Cannons?"

"They use whatever they can find. They throw rocks, they throw books, they throw people, they throw . . . anything."

"Is that the people that know that do this?"

"Oh, no! People that know know better than that."

"Are they peaceful and loving?"

"Yes."

"Do the animal people come in and destroy houses when you build them?"

"Yes."

"Do you destroy any of the ones that don't know?"

"Oh, I would like to sometimes."

"Are they destroyed ever?"

"Yes."

"But their population continues to increase?"

"Oh, yes. They're like animals. They fight a lot and they have more of the same animals and they're so many of them. They fight amongst each other. That's how some of them get killed, most of them."

"What do they do?"

"Plus, they're just stupid. They do stupid things."

"Do they only eat, procreate, and fight?"

"Yeah, just about."

"How long does it take a child to be born with them?"

"Well, it's the same as everybody else."

"Do you have such things as marriages with the people that know . . . mates?"

"With the people that know, yes, but you don't mean marriages with the people that don't know."

"Oh no no no no no. I'm talking strictly within the people that know now. Do you live in a house?"

"Mm-hmh."

"Do you have a family? Or anybody that you live with?"

"I live with other people."

"Is it a large building?"

"No, it's much easier to keep a small one."

"How are the houses? What are they built out of?"

"They're of a kind of stone, a mix of a lot of stones. There are many of them that are put together. It's a hybrid stone. It's very strong and the houses are molded in shape and the ones that have managed to last are very nice. They're very beautiful. They have very sleek lines."

"What do you use to heat? Do you have any power of any kind for heat and light?"

"We have some other stones that radiate light."

"How are they made?"

"That I don't know. I'm not involved in that. They're somewhat natural but you have to find them and then there's a process that they do."

"I see."

"They have a glow."

"Can you read by them?"

"Yes."

"What part of the world are you living in now based on the geography as it exists in your present incarnation? Are you someplace in Europe or in what is now in the United States or in the Far East or Africa or where?"

"It's in the very middle of the United States."

"Does the United States exist anymore?"

"Mmmm . . . no. Not that old United States."

"Do you have a one-world government now?"

"That's a big issue. Between the people that know, that's the biggest issue. One of the biggest issues. The other thing, of course, is dealing with the people that don't know."

"Would you be better off to destroy all the people that don't know?"

"No!"

"What do they contribute?"

"Not much yet, but they will. They have to learn."

"Are they capable of learning?"

"Well, sometimes I doubt it but I think eventually, yes. I have to do my part."

"I see. What do you eat? Where do you get your food from?"

"We try to grow it. And we try to manufacture it."

"How do you manufacture it?"

"It's very difficult."

"Are you living in what would be called a city?"

"Yes."

"What is the name of that city?"

"Tertonia."

"Do you enjoy your life at all?"

"It's very hard. It's hard. Actually you know, the people that don't know are sometimes very funny. In a way I know I shouldn't laugh at them but they don't realize how funny they are."

"Do they look just like you except that they're not educated or is there a difference in appearance?"

"Yeah, they're real different."

"In what way? What do you look like? Do you have a mirror that you can look at yourself in?"

"Well, I'm wearing a kind of robe and it's the robe that the people that teach wear and it's long and it's grey. It has a lavender border around the bottom and up the middle where it comes together. It makes a pyramid shape as I wear it which is one of the reasons that I wear it."

"How do you travel around the city or if you go from one city to another? Can you do that?"

"Oh, yes."

"What's your means of transportation?"

"Oh, we go in the bubbles . . . "

"I see."

"Usually."

"What do the bubbles look like and what moves them?"

"The bubbles are like plastic and there are different kinds. There are kinds that operate entirely mechanically and there are kinds that operate mentally. They look very similar but the mental ones take much more effort to run around in because you have to concentrate. It's almost impossible to use them too because unless you go high, the people that don't know are always shooting at them."

"Mm-hmh! Do they go very fast?"

"Mm-hmh."

"The people that don't know are shooting at them."

"Why are they shooting at them?"

"Oh, anything they can find to shoot. If you're low down, they'll shoot rocks or anything. If you're far up, they'll try to scavenge all the old ancient weapons and try to make 'em work."

"Are you vegetarians?"

"Yes."

"Do you eat meat at all?"

"No."

"Do you have plenty of food?"

"The people that don't know eat meat. Some of them eat each other."

"All right. You're eighteen years of age. Anything else you'd like to tell me?"

"No."

"Well, let's move forward to where you're twenty-two years of age. On the count of three, without any stress or strain. One . . . two . . . three. Where are you now? Still a teacher?"

"Yes."

"Same place?"

"Yes, except I'm doing slightly different teaching. I've decided that you can't teach across such a gap."

"Mm-hmh!"

"And I've decided that I have to do a kind of a disguise of being like one of the people that don't know. So I disguise myself. Then I try to act real crude and I think it's working."

"Can't they tell the difference in your appearance—your physical appearance?"

"Oh, I've disguised that."

"I see."

"I like the little ones."

"They're the easiest to teach, aren't they?"

"Yeah. I don't mind their being so . . . crude. It's when they grow up and they're still crude it bothers me."

"Do they speak a language you can understand?"

"Well, we speak the same language but it doesn't

have the same meaning for them."

"Can you speak some of the language to me? If you were going to give a little bit of a lecture on how to clean yourself or do something like that, tell me what you would say in that language?"

"Are you one of the people that know?"

"Would you use English, the same language you speak in your present incarnation?" Tom paused. "Talk to me in the tongue as if you were talking to somebody who is not in the know and trying to teach them. What would the language sound like?"

"From just talking as I would."

In my present mind, I was surprised at Tom's request. He hadn't asked in any other lives for me to speak to him in the vernacular. Regardless of the past life, I always spoke in American English which might vary slightly in tone and use of slang and grammar, depending on the particular past life.

I would have been curious myself to hear the language of this bizarre future society but it didn't come out. It may be that here and in the past lives too, I was speaking in the vernacular but my present conscious mind automatically translated everything into modern American English to answer Tom's questions. So when I said I was "talking as I would," it may have meant that the future life mind actually was directing speech in the future language but was somehow unaware that the speech was being changed into American English in order to make sense in the present. This mechanistic explanation is just a guess, assuming of course, that there were indeed these past and future lives.

"All right. You're now twenty-two years old and you're working with the people. Do you sleep with them and eat with them? Or do you go back to your own house at night? Hmm?" Whenever there was a long pause as there was now, Tom gently pursued his questioning.

"You're seeing or feeling something. Can you tell me? What is going on? Syzzyx, can you tell me, please?"

"It's gone."

"The life is gone?"

"Mm-hmh."

"Ask Fortune if we should go back to it. What does he say?"

"He says, 'That's all you need to know.'"

"Okay. That's fine. What was it you were supposed to learn in this?"

"He says, 'Don't be afraid to lead others even if they don't see the rightness of what you see.' That's the lesson. He says I'm not used to the idea of thinking of myself as a leader. He says the kind of leading people are used to is going to be different from now on. There's a different kind of movement. He says, if there's anything else, that I can always write to him. I could be writing to him more but it's good that, at least, I'm working on the book. He's going back in his rock and he's saying that should be enough for today. Finish it quickly."

Tom carried on with the usual exit procedure to bring me back gradually to my present and awake state of mind. As I regained normal consciousness, my reaction to the future lifetime was, curiously, as unemotional as the life itself. What little emotion there was left was limited to mild amusement and a mere suggestion of exasperation.

I wondered if the lack of feeling was because I supposedly hadn't really lived out that life as yet, because I was temperamentally an unemotional person in that life, or because I just didn't take the idea of seeing a future life seriously and therefore didn't acknowledge any feelings associated with it. But I didn't care to explore the matter further. It was not an easy life for me from what I saw and I didn't look forward to it if, in fact, I would eventually have to live it out.

It did have its humorous side though. The people that didn't know were funny. They made me think of hedgehogs—small, round creatures that just bumped haphazardly up against each other and life in general. Just the idea of looking at a future life was amusing enough and I was content to enjoy that. I didn't feel the need to fuss over any heavy-duty lessons. After all, I still supposedly had that life to live.

Of course that was a big issue in itself because it brought up the old question of predestination versus free will—a question that was not answered by just looking at a supposedly future life. After all, if the very reason for bothering to look at past lives was to change one's direction from this point forward, then one could also alter between now and then any particular future scenario. I toyed with the idea that only physical events might be foreordained and the non-physical emotions and attitudes concerning those events might be subject to change. But emotions and behavior are too intermingled for that scheme to make sense. The only resolution to the dilemma was the acknowledgment that our normal limitations of space and time just didn't function in the bigger picture.

Nevertheless, Fortune said there was a lesson to be learned about leadership. It seemed that my current ideas on leadership, and about my being a leader, needed some re-examination. I tend to keep a mental picture of many issues as lining themselves up either horizontally or vertically on an imaginary gyroscope of sorts. The horizontal disc represents a circle of sharing, communal egalitarianism as contrasted to the vertical axis that represents a hierarchical ladder of competitive, individual authoritarianism. Such activities as getting together with friends would be horizontal; beating someone else out of a job promotion would be vertical. My bias is obvious. The horizontal is more comfortable, more friendly, more peaceful.

Before this session, the very idea of leadership, as far as I was concerned, always lined up on the vertical axis and therefore was less productive. But Fortune was hinting at a new way of looking at leadership that might not be so problematic, although the full sense of that lesson was elusive.

So there I was at the last of these sessions. I was continuing the dialogues with Fortune on my own. These were valuable and would have been even more so if I could have dispensed with my doubts and taken full advantage of his excellent guidance and wisdom. And Fortune had made it clear that I should be compiling a book—this book—of all the transcriptions of the past-life sessions. So I worked on these various tasks simultaneously. I conversed with Fortune at the keyboard. I transcribed and put the past-life sessions in order. And I continued to try to understand the ultimate purpose of all these journeys.

I looked back at the sessions. Each had its own tone and at least one general theme or issue that were sometimes different from the original purpose for embarking on each session.

The Mexican lifetime as Rita was first. After my brother's fatal accident in that life, the life became a melancholy one of self-pity until, near the end, I was finally able to forget myself enough to turn outward to help others, discovering in the process the pleasure of doing so. If indeed one lives past lives that end with unresolved issues being carried over into subsequent lifetimes, the Mexican life may have provided the impetus, the unconscious motivations, for my preschool teaching, childbirth teaching and astrology work in this lifetime. It could be that issues that remained unresolved from past lives sought resolution in subsequent lives. I was made to feel responsible for my little brother's death in the Mexico life and felt I was somehow punished by not being able to have a happily married life with children. This time around, I trained in and taught mothers about childbirth and also trained in and taught early childhood education. Curiously, the early childhood education was based on the Montessori method, which resembled some of the Atlantis training.

It could also be that people or activities that were part of a past life showed up again in some form for the sake of comfortable familiarity, not as a problem to be resolved but as a continuation or further development. The end of the Mexico past life involved my looking at the stars and telling people useful things as a result. I was not a trained astrologer then but, taking it a step further in my present lifetime, I learned formally about astrology and therefore could draw up and read people's birthcharts.

More significantly, that first session challenged my view of reality. I wavered between wanting to believe that the Mexican life was indeed a life I had lived and then doubting it all. The issue of doubt and belief was an undercurrent throughout all the past-life explorations and the subsequent dialoguing with the spirit guide Fortune. That session, being the first, expanded my view of reality beyond birth and death to a larger cosmic picture.

From shy Rita, there was a complete about-face to boisterous outspoken Susan of the English lifetime. My focus in that life was definitely outward and my great desire was to travel and find adventure. Circumstances in my present lifetime have allowed for the kind of travel I was apparently aching for as Susan. When I was only seventeen in my present lifetime, I traveled around the world for a year in an unusual school, the International School of America, begun by a man, Karl Jaeger, who believed strongly that young people should travel and learn. It was an amazing experience that included home stays with local families in Japan, India, Lebanon, Egypt, Turkey, Greece, Italy, and elsewhere and meetings with remarkable world leaders like Malcolm X and Prime Minister Nehru of India. In the past life, fear thwarted my journey to India but as I would never admit it, I projected it on to others finding fault everywhere but in myself. My death in that life which was due to drowning just might explain my eagerness to learn how to swim early in this life. But the drowning was really due to arguing, endless arguing, with my husband. Perhaps this is why this time around I have sought harder for more peaceful means of resolving conflict.

Curiously, I got a kick out of reliving the life as "Fireball," the feisty redhead Susan. I liked her gutsy approach and enjoyed the thought of her in me. In the days following the session, I found myself feeling more rambunctious. But Susan's way of striving for independence was by railing against other people. The trick seems to be to keep her gusto and, at the same time, a commitment to peacemaking.

The third past-life session with Sister Elizabeth was the most intense, emotional experience—an experience of deep connection. It was a great lesson in the power of love to make an otherwise unwanted life livable. If Sister Elizabeth is indeed my son in my present lifetime, it might help to explain the strong bond we have. But this past-life explanation is not one that needs further pursuing at this time, given Fortune's advice.

The life in early Greece as a sandal-maker was a

good life of simple pleasures. It was the first past life I experienced as a man, which gave it a unique quality of its own. I cannot say for sure if what it felt like to be a man in that life would translate to being a man in any life. It seemed that my concerns were those of what we think of as a traditional masculine role. The original intent was to seek out a connection to a friend, Clark, in my current life. The effect was that I felt released from a hidden compulsion to follow in his footsteps and, instead, felt a sense of freedom to follow my own path wherever it might lead.

The very early life was a lesson about survival and relationship to others as a prerequisite for survival. Also, this past life, more than any other, stretched the gap between a past-life mind and my present mind. It was difficult to jump back and forth between that extremely unsophisticated existence and the present. Brains just didn't seem to work the same way then. This raised questions in me about the nature and evolution of the mind over thousands of years and how time-bound our current notion of intelligence seems to be. Going so far back into prehistory, I felt as if I had traced the roots of an enormous tree down through countless layers of dark, rich, life-giving soil to bedrock. From that depth emerged the vision of an interconnected human family and the need for us to help each other for survival. I had felt personally a past stretching so far back in time that it had the effect of making life now feel all the grander for such a rich foundation of hundreds of years before it.

The solitary life as Pieter, the calligrapher,

demonstrated that a source, or perhaps the ultimate source, of creativity is divine inspiration. The session also set the course for my new kind of writing, which was now to focus on the content of writing rather than on the beauty of the letter forms. In this present life, I have studied calligraphy and done calligraphy work. For the sake of learning calligraphy, I travelled back to Japan where I had spent time during that year in the round-the-world school. I taught English there but on my own time studied Japanese calligraphy with a wonderful older woman teacher. Doing calligraphy in my present life then seemed like a continuation or elaboration on what I, as Pieter, had done before. But calligraphy work has not continued. Instead the writing recently has been for the sake of its content rather than the look of letter forms on the page. Having contact with spirits then also set the stage for what was turning out to be another act, the conversations with Fortune, in an ongoing drama.

I also experienced in one session (not included) looking back at my own childhood in this lifetime. This session had the effect of reinforcing my belief in the truth of the other sessions. I knew these childhood memories to be correct so the past-life memories began looking equally believable. Also, it brought up issues of biological family connection as opposed to one's own soul inheritance. As a result I realized that a person could trace two separate lineages—first, a biological line to your family ancestors; second, a spiritual line to your former existences.

The session that was an extended conversation with

Fortune paved the way for the conversations with Fortune I began to engage in more seriously after completing the past-life explorations and without the help of hypnosis.

The past life in Jerusalem, the result of seeking a possible past-life connection with my mother in this present life, revolved more overtly around spiritual, or, at least, religious issues. As Orcus, I tried to figure out who had the truth. The search may have started in that lifetime but it did not end there. In fact, experiencing what it was like to live at the beginning of the Christian era with the variety of belief systems extant widened the possible range of spiritual beliefs.

The Atlantis lifetime took my understanding a step further. Even though chronologically the Atlantis life would have preceded the Jerusalem life, I encountered the Jerusalem life first. The past life in Greece had involved accepting my own way of life in the world as equally valid as any other while the past life in Atlantis had shown that while one must progress at one's own pace it must not be at the expense of others. If one chooses a solitary path, one's actions or thoughts can still affect others. Even a small stone dropped in one side of a lake can send waves to the other shore.

Lastly, the future life tried to answer the question, Where do we go from here? But this life was to me the most suspect. For one thing, it seemed so one-dimensional, almost cartoon-like. For another thing, it was hard to get a sense of exact time or place. For yet another thing, I couldn't really fathom how I could see a future life or learn from something that hadn't even happened as yet.

But the issue of leadership that arose in that lifetime was definitely worth thinking about.

At times in working with Tom, I wondered about his only guiding the sessions and not delving more into the meaning of the issues that came up. When I asked him about this, he said that he was always available for discussion but did not initiate it. He thought the process of understanding what content emerged would be better directed by the person involved. In addition, assimilation might take anywhere from minutes to months to years. To sit just after a past-life session with the intention of sorting it all out then and there might yield some clarification. However, answers do not always come so neatly and quickly. Tom insisted that the sessions were only to set up the work that the person must do on his or her own. He was quite correct in this as discoveries and more discoveries continue to emerge from these visited lives. In fact, a lesson of the Atlantis lifetime was the importance of patience in the process of learning.

In addition, Tom didn't try himself to live past lives for someone else and then report on his findings. He saw more value in having each person re-experience for herself or himself the past life. Second-hand information may be of some benefit but the vividness of perception and the immediacy of emotion experienced first-hand would have a much greater impact. Also, seeing as much of a life as possible from youth to death can allow one to learn not only certain lessons but the context in which those lessons arose

The past lives separately and together offered

much in the way of learning and experience. There were obvious superficial connections to my present life and connections between one or another of the past lives themselves. However, there were deeper issues as well which became apparent more slowly and are still forthcoming. There would surely be more drama if I were able to say that, as a direct result of doing all these sessions, my personal life changed radically. It didn't.

The greatest change on the personal level has been subtle and difficult to contain in neat before and after pictures. One lesson has been to acknowledge the power of trust, which is to say, faith. At the heart of the various past-life adventures and my conversations with Fortune was my struggle between doubt and faith. I was drawn into these adventures partly by circumstance and partly by curiosity. In the process, I learned that one can also proceed by faith in that which is both beyond oneself and within oneself but not always immediately apparent to oneself. One must allow for mystery and patiently allow whatever might emerge to emerge.

These explorations also taught an epistemological lesson—that there is more than one way of coming to knowledge. And some forms of knowing have their own intrinsic truth whether or not there is verification externally by other ways of knowing.

I have been fortunate to have been guided to consider life beyond the limits of birth and death. It feels like stepping out of a stuffy house into the cool black of night and gazing into a starry sky, the mystery and sheer wondrous immensity of which makes the least surge of life on this little planet all the more precious.

Epilogue

You may be wondering how knowing all these past lives changed my present life. Certainly the lives themselves— the glimpses of afterlife, and Fortune as a spirit guide— all jostled my own world view.

Fortune said he could see my quandary about whether or not to believe the past lives as real. He suggested two ways for me to test their reality. One way was to try to verify any testable facts gleaned from the past lives. The other way was to live with them all and allow the truth to emerge in its own time.

At first, I was eager to verify what details I could. I looked at maps of 18th century Mexico. I looked at business listings of 19th century London. I tried to track distances between Mainz, Germany and Rheims, France for what travel would mean there in the 17th century. But aside from such factual details, there was a clear emotional truth to each of the lives. I believed them even if I could not explain how they happened.

Although I attempted to verify factual content of the past lives, there were not many facts to go on. However, Fortune's second path for finding truth—allowing the truth to emerge on its own in its own time—has been life-altering.

I felt the need to learn more, and my wanting to learn drew me to wonder about the origins of religion. At the time, many people made a clear and insistent distinction between religion and spirituality. Religion meant the organized institutions of churches, temples, mosques with all their texts and rituals whereas spirituality referred to more individual searches for purpose and meaning beyond the familiar seen world. I decided I wanted to go back to school to study this.

In the 1980s I began a master's program in the history and phenomenology of religion at the Graduate Theological Union in Berkeley, California. My intent was to study the origin of the religious impulse both in the evolution of humanity and in the life course of any one individual. Somehow the scope of my questioning seemed to keep widening. What I wrote as a result of those years of study was titled "The Necessity of Wilderness" where wilderness did not stop at its biblical meaning but expanded to include metaphorically all that which is beyond what we know. Certainly I'd had a glimpse into worlds beyond what I knew with the past-life explorations.

When in one past-life session, Tom Thomason asked Fortune what the purpose of my present life was, Fortune answered that "it touches many parts of the world" with travel of a metaphorical kind and a lot of writing about the "mysteries of life."

Later, when we began a session with a plan to look into a past life for sources of creativity, Fortune directed us to the one with Pieter the calligrapher. Fortune said again that I would, in my current life, be doing much writing but that it would not be "the usual kind of writing." Rather that it would bring in "a lot of different things including writing and designing the way people think about the world."

He presented me with an image of papers and papers full of writing. Fortune predicted correctly. That is what has happened. Fortune also directed me to begin a dialogue with him on my own. Even though I was hesitant at first, this dialogue became a form of channeling. Fortune said that my writing wasn't going to be what he called pretty writing.

"Pretty writing is your hobby now, not your work."

I supposed at the time that by "pretty writing" he meant the calligraphy that Pieter was doing in the church. However, some years ago when I retired from teaching anthropology, I was drawn back to my childhood love of poetry. I started writing poetry, completing several publications. However, it occurs to me now that poetry, at least as I was writing it, may also have been the "pretty writing" Fortune was referring to as hobby, not my real work.

Here is what happened next. After writing poetry for some time, I remembered having done these past-life explorations under hypnosis. I wondered whether I might use hypnotic trance for poetry, for generating new poems. I found another hypnotist to test this out and got into a regular practice of inducing trance and writing while in trance. The trance writing soon morphed into automatic writing where I would instruct my hand to write on its own. Sometimes I was aware of what my hand was writing; other times I didn't know what my hand had written until I came out of the trance.

To my surprise, the voices of people I knew who had died started showing up on the written pages. And then other voices. Before I realized it, I was doing a sort of channeling very similar to my earlier dialogues with Fortune. I remembered the lesson Fortune gave me when I mysteriously became a rock—the lesson that was intended to show me a way of losing myself to become a channel. All this has unfolded over many years and much of it can be traced back to what Fortune spoke of in the midst of the past-life sessions.

On the issue of love and relationships, Fortune predicted that I would remarry—and "sooner than I would have expected." I didn't have any expectations at all at that time. The men I had been dating when doing the past-life work were pleasant companions but not what I considered marriage partners. However, within a year of Fortune's prediction, when I enrolled in the masters program in religion I met a man there who soon became my husband. So there too, Fortune's prediction was correct. Fortune had wisdom and foresight that has borne itself out even though when he made these various pronouncements, I hardly thought them credible.

These days I divide my writing time between poetry, automatic writing in trance, and channeling spiritual entities who borrow my voice to deliver messages. Ah, but that is a conversation for another day.

Acknowledgements

This book of past-life stories has been made possible by a number of people. I am especially grateful to Nina Alvarez of Cosmographia Books. I thank her and her staff for the editing, design, and cover art and for her expertise, patience, and enthusiasm from start to finish.

I also wish to thank those who wrote such kind endorsements of the book. I know how much this work has meant to me so it is gratifying to see that it has resonated with others as well.

Early readers included the women of the Feminist Research Group in the Lehigh Valley (PA) who aside from their high interest in the stories, encouraged and confirmed me as a "trustworthy narrator." I also wish to thank Renni Browne for her even earlier editorial suggestions.

My sister, Tamsin, has been a very special reader with thoughtful comments from start to finish. I treasure her ongoing support.

None of this would have been possible without those who have since passed into spirit—my friend, Andrew, who started me on these journeys years ago, and the hypnotist Tom Thomason who conducted the many hours these sessions consumed. Whoever Fortune was, is, or will continue to be, I am grateful for his otherworldly guidance throughout.

And last, special thanks to my dear husband, Bruce, who has been the most magnificent life partner.

About the Author

Elizabeth Bodien is the author of two books of poetry: *Blood, Metal, Fiber, Rock* and *Oblique Music: A Book of Hours.* Her poems, essays, and book reviews have appeared in *Cimarron Review, Crannóg,* and *Parabola,* among many other publications in the USA, Ireland, Canada, Australia, and India. Bodien holds degrees in cultural anthropology, consciousness studies, religions, and poetry, and has worked as an instructor of English in Japan, an organic farmer in the mountains of Oregon, a childbirth instructor in Ghana, West Africa, and as a professor of anthropology. Bodien grew up in the "burned-over" district of Western New York but now lives near Hawk Mountain, Pennsylvania.